GARDENING TIME
THE FLOWER GARDEN

GEOFF AMOS

CENTRAL

Boxtree

First published Great Britain in 1988 by Boxtree Limited

Copyright © Central Independent Television plc, 1988

ISBN 1 85283 228 2

Line drawings by Mei Lim
Designed by Groom and Pickerill
Typeset by York House Typographic
Printed in Italy by New Interlitho Spâ, Milan.
for Boxtree Limited
36 Tavistock Street
London
WC2E 7PB

The author and publishers thank Asmer Seeds Ltd for photographs on pp 30, 67, 72
and Sutton Seeds Ltd for photographs on pp 15, 32, 60, 65, 70, 73

CONTENTS

PREFACE

The Gardening Time programme was started in 1972 as a weekly feature and since then has continued to be produced 52 weeks of the year.

The garden is situated in a Birmingham park in the suburb of Kings Heath. The first two presenters of the programme, Cyril Fletcher and the late Bob Price, created from a piece of waste ground a superb garden of just over one-third of an acre which contained a rockery, waterfall and pool, island beds, paved areas, a small vegetable garden, a small soft fruit garden and the typical 8×20 greenhouse.

In 1983, the City of Birmingham Parks and Amenities Department gave permission to extend the garden to 7 acres. Work began on a adjacent site and to date we have created over 1½ acres of new gardens with different styles of landscape. There is also an extended vegetable garden with organic and non-organic trial bed areas, a large herb garden, and trial beds for roses, dahlias, chrysanthemums and bedding plants – all propagated from three new greenhouses.

The four expert presenters of the Gardening Time programme are Arthur Billitt (fruit and vegetables), Jock Davidson (house plants), Geoff Amos (all-round gardening, especially bedding plants) and Howard Drury (alpines, conifers, heathers, shrubs) who is also the programme's Horticultural Adviser.

The programme spans the entire year and these accompanying books show how, by doing the right things at the right time, anybody can become a successful amateur gardener.

JOHN PULLEN
PRODUCER

INTRODUCTION

This book is not aimed at the experienced gardener or the experts. They can be expected to know the answers to the problems that often beset the ordinary enthusiast, and sometimes completely fox the beginner – problems such as which flowers will live for only one season and which will keep coming up every year unattended, which have to be grown from seeds, and which are best grown from cuttings, or division of roots, or from bulbs.

They will know the tough ones that will live outside all the time, and those that should be dug up or otherwise protected from winter frosts.

They will know too, whether particular kinds like sunshine or shade, wet or dry, heavy or light ground, how long they will last, what colour and height they are, and their season of flowering.

Some of them might even know a string of those tiresome but necessary Latin names by which all our plants are listed and distinguished.

You may be sure, nevertheless, that not even the expert knows it all, not even all about just this one aspect of gardening garden flowers. We all live and learn, and keep on learning. Don't be worried. There are hundreds of thousands of magnificent front and back gardens throughout the country, large and small, planted and tended by folk who do not know or care that a daisy is *Bellis perennis* or a nasturtium *Tropaeolum majus*, and who have found out, by trial and error, that marigolds like sunshine better than shade, and dahlias generally die if you leave them in the ground through the winter.

They will have tried and failed in some years, and tried and triumphed in others. But they have kept on trying, and kept on learning – helped at times by books, magazines, articles, radio and television programmes.

To know it however, you have to do it. There is no substitute for experience at gardening.

Your patch won't suddenly turn into a blaze of colour

just because you have read this book; but if you are prepared to help yourself, it will guide you along the interesting and joyful path of the flower garden.

GEOFF AMOS

As a handy cross-reference for calculating plant dimensions, planting depths and distances, etc., where mentioned in the text, the following list gives approximate metric equivalents to imperial measurements.

½ in	1 cm	18 in	45 cm
1 in	2.5 cm	20 in	50 cm
2 in	5 cm	24 in	60 cm
3 in	7.5 cm	30 in	75 cm
4 in	10 cm	36 in	90 cm
5 in	13 cm	4 ft	1.2 m
6 in	15 cm	5 ft	1.5 m
7 in	18 cm	6 ft	1.8 m
8 in	20 cm	7 ft	2.1 m
9 in	23 cm	8 ft	2.4 m
10 in	25 cm	9 ft	2.7 m
11 in	28 cm	10 ft	3 m
12 in	30 cm	12 ft	3.6 m
15 in	38 cm	15 ft	4.5 m

1. LIFE CYCLES

The countless different flowers in our gardens have many different fads and fancies regarding soils and situations; but by listing together those that have the same life-cycles, they can conveniently be classified into groups. Once we know to which group a plant belongs, we have a good idea of its basic needs, although it may have special likes and dislikes which must be considered if we are to grow it well.

We divide them first, then, by their life-spans. The principal divisions, based on life-spans, are:

---

1. *Annuals* – which live for just one year.
2. *Biennials* – which live for two years.
3. *Perennials* – which live almost indefinitely.

In this country, however, the year is divided into two very distinct periods as far as plant life is concerned: approximately from October to mid-May, when the temperature is likely to fall below 32°F (0°C), and from about mid-May to October, when there is unlikely to be any frost. Some plants, generally natives, are able to shrug off the effects of frost, others originating in warmer countries are killed or at least severely damaged by it.

This is of great importance to the gardener, and because of it, each of the three principal groups has to be subdivided into plants that are capable of withstanding frost, known as *hardy*, and those that are not, known as *half-hardy*.

There are thus six groups:

---

1. *Hardy annuals* (HA) e.g. nasturtiums
2. *Half-hardy annuals* (HHA) e.g. French marigolds
3. *Hardy biennials* (HB) e.g. Canterbury bells
4. *Half-hardy biennials* (HHB) e.g. many greenhouse plants
5. *Hardy perennials* (HP) e.g. Michaelmas daisies
6. *Half-hardy perennials* (HHP) e.g. dahlias

All the garden flowers we grow fall into one or the other of these groups.

Even with this information, however, it is not immediately clear, for example, whether new seeds have to be sown for another year, whether plants can be left to grow again the following season, or whether plants should be dug up and taken inside for protection. With such uncertainties in mind, I have listed these six groups in a slightly different way, putting plants into just four categories. They are:

Category One
Flowers that have to be started afresh from seeds every year, i.e. hardy annuals, half-hardy annuals, hardy biennials, and half-hardy biennials.

Category Two
Flowers that are left in the ground permanently, and keep coming up every year, i.e. hardy perennials.

Category Three
Flowers that have to be dug up in the autumn for protection, and planted again in the spring, i.e. half-hardy perennials.

Category Four
Flowers from bulbs and corms. These could be listed with the perennials, but it is more convenient for them to be in a separate group.

2. CHARACTERISTICS OF ANNUALS AND BIENNIALS (CATEGORY ONE)

Annuals and biennials are as pretty and colourful as any. Their great value, however, is the speed at which they grow and produce their flowers. The fact that a packet of seeds chosen from the rack in a shop or a garden centre in the spring, perhaps as late as April, or even May, can be sown, grown and be in full glorious bloom in the garden by July and August, has obvious appeal, particularly for the new gardener and for the very young, who need action and speedy results to keep them interested and enthusiastic.

A short life
Speed, however, has its drawbacks. It is a headlong gallop towards death. Our fleeting spring and summer is their whole lifetime, and their aim is simply to flower and produce their seeds as quickly as possible. This is nature's way of making sure the species is perpetuated.

For years it has been one of the objectives of plant breeders to raise new strains and varieties with as long a flowering life as possible. Much has been done along these lines recently with the introduction of F1 and F2 hybrid varieties of many popular favourites. As well as giving new colours, sizes and shapes, these are not quite so intent on producing seeds, and therefore flower over a longer period than their older counterparts. Some of the newer French and African marigolds are classic examples.

Many of these superb newcomers, coming into flower as early as June from a March sowing, will still be giving a colourful display when the frosts come in October, sometimes lasting into November.

Hardy annuals
Hardy annuals (HAs), as the description implies, are hardy enough for their seeds to be sown direct into the open ground, from February to April, while there is still a possibility of frost. Clarkia, godetia and candytuft are well known examples.

Half-hardy annuals
Half-hardy annuals (HHAs) need sowing at the same time, but are not hardy enough to be sown outside. The warmth of a greenhouse in February and March, and the protection of a cold frame in April, are needed to raise plants that are ready to set outside in their flowering positions from mid-May onwards, when the likelihood of frost has gone.

These HHAs are the popular 'bedding out' plants, sold by the million in punnets, boxes, trays, etc. in garden centres, shops and nurseries, and raised in small greenhouses.

Stocks, asters, alyssum and nemesia are among many easily grown popular kinds.

Godetia, a popular hardy annual.

Exceptions to the rule

Despite these general observations, there are two exceptional cases that deserve mentioning because they are often confusing to beginners.

The first exception relates to annuals. Although these grow, live, flower and die within twelve months, those twelve months need not occur in the same year.

With some kinds it is possible to sow seeds, not in the spring, as is normal, to flower the same year, but in late August or early September, for flowering the following year. These germinate and grow into small plants in the autumn, remaining this size in a semi-dormant state through the winter, to grow away in the spring and flower earlier than usual. In addition, they tend to

grow bigger and better than normal, because of the extra time they have had to build up a large root system.

It is a method much favoured by growers of sweet peas for exhibition, who, by sowing the seeds in October, thereby gain the extra length of stem and size of flower needed to win prizes at the shows. Larkspur and cornflowers, when long stems are required for cutting, can also be grown this way.

The second exception concerns perennials which are grown and used like half-hardy annuals, as one-year bedding plants. They include well known flowers such as antirrhinums, begonias, seed-raised geraniums and busy lizzies.

The distinction is made in

catalogues and on seed packets, which carry the instruction 'Treat as HHAs', which means sow and grow them as if they were just one-season plants.

With care, and luck, some will go on from one year to another – as in the case of antirrhinums – but they are more reliable raised afresh every year from new seeds.

When growing and entering annuals for exhibition, however, be careful not to include any of these perennials 'treated as half-hardy annuals', as judges will probably disqualify them.

Biennials

Although biennials have been included in Category One, they occupy something of a grey area. The term is used not so much to describe the life-cycle of the plant, as to indicate the way it is grown. For instance, wallflowers and sweet williams are invariably listed and grown as hardy biennials – sown one year to flower the next – when they are really perennials. An odd plant or two may sometimes live on for years if left undisturbed in a favourable situation, but this characteristic is so unreliable that they are best disposed of after flowering, and new plants raised. True biennials, in fact, do not feature prominently among our garden plants, either in hardy or half-hardy form. Honesty and Canterbury bells are two of the most common, both of them suitable for the small garden.

Canterbury bells, one of few true hardy biennials.

3. HARDY ANNUALS (CATEGORY ONE)

Because it is in their nature to produce their seeds readily, and in comparatively large quantities, hardy annuals in seed packets are generally inexpensive. Because of this, and their rapid and easy growth, they are invaluable for quickly covering the ground, over large areas if necessary, and giving colour in a new garden.

They are particularly useful for filling the spaces that are bound to exist before the more permanent plants take over. Gaps between newly-planted shrubs, and spaced-out herbaceous plants, or unoccupied pockets on rockeries, can all be cheaply and easily filled with hardy annuals as a temporary measure.

Even window boxes, tubs, urns and hanging baskets can be sown with these accommodating flowers, if carefully chosen.

There are types to suit almost any situation. Some reach an impressive height of 3–4 ft in their short season; others have stems of 18–24 in and are good for cutting; and many make low-growing bushes covered with bloom. Incredibly, too, considering their short life, there are trailers, and even climbers.

The most inexpensive way of buying them is as 'mixtures' when almost anything can be included. These are particularly recommended for large areas, perhaps as a temporary measure for beds or borders that will eventually be planted with more lasting subjects. They can also go into the 'wild' garden, where the seeds can be scattered at random without any set pattern or plan, left to seed themselves and come up in even greater numbers the following year.

For specific controlled places, it is better to buy separate varieties, or even a single variety, on the basis of height, habit and, if need be, colour.

Although uncommon, a bed or border composed exclusively of hardy annuals can be an attractive feature, even in an established garden.

For this it is advisable to choose separate varieties, looking to create good colour combinations, good contrasts of upright growing and spreading plants, and different plant heights.

A plan drawn on paper beforehand is a great help. Mark out areas of different shapes and sizes for each kind, and then choose those you think will go well together and look the best.

Hardy annuals for cutting

If you want hardy annuals for cut flowers, it may be useful to grow them separately for this specific purpose.

Sweet peas, very widely grown in rows, are, of course, the classic example; but a row, say, of long-stemmed clarkia, cornflower or larkspur, across the vegetable patch, will provide cut flowers by the armful over several weeks in

Lavateras are good for garden decoration and cutting.

the summer, for a very modest outlay and very little trouble. This can be a great convenience for flower arrangers, in particular, for such a scheme will take nothing away from the purely decorative part of the flower garden.

Trailing and climbing hardy annuals

These are not very numerous, simply because they have to be grown very fast indeed to be effective in their one short season of growth.

Sweet peas, with their grasping tendrils, are the obvious climbers, and the shorter varieties of these, such as 'Jet Set', 'Knee-high' and 'Snoopea', can be used as trailers. The nasturtium family, too, has varieties that can be used either way.

The near-nasturtium relation *Tropaeolum peregrinum* (canary creeper), is the most rapid of all; given a hedge or comparable support to cling to, it may reach 10–12 ft in a season.

Saving seeds

As a general rule, the dying flowers should be picked off hardy annuals to prevent seed formation, thereby to some extent prolonging the flowering period. But it is quite easy to gather seeds to keep and sow the following season. They must be left on the plant to ripen, and in some cases have to be carefully watched, because they may be quickly shed and drop to the ground. If gathered when dry, labelled (very important because names are easily forgotten), stored in envelopes and kept dry

through the winter, they will germinate and grow reliably in the spring. Although the colours may not be exactly the same as the plants they came from, they will still produce a colourful – and free – display in the summer.

Soil requirements

Most annuals will be unbalanced and make too much leaf growth if sown in rich soil or in shady places. A sunny open spot in full light, and in ground with no special manuring or fertilising, will give the best results, although if it dries out too quickly, the life of the flowers is shortened.

The texture of the top inch or so is more important than its fertility; and although ground should always be loosened with a fork, the surface must be capable of being raked down finely so that the seedlings, often very small, are not prevented from coming through by large lumps of soil or stones. A scattering of fine peat, or peat and sand, before sowing is beneficial, particularly on heavy or newly dug soil.

The exception to the non-manuring rule is the sweet pea. These are particularly deep rooting, and it is almost standard practice to prepare a trench or

special spot for them, by digging in manure or compost. They will certainly respond to good treatment, both in quality and quantity of flower. If you specialise, dig out, each year, a trench 24 in wide and 24 in or more deep, and fill it with well mixed manure and soil, and finish by adding to the surface a balanced fertiliser such as 'Growmore', at 2 oz to the yard run (55g per metre). A simpler procedure is to fork some well-rotted manure or compost into the top 9 in or so, plus the surface fertiliser dressing.

Spring sowing

Most hardy annual seeds are best sown outside, directly into the precise places where they are intended to grow and flower. Since they are generally too small to put in singly, they are scattered thinly over the area to be covered. In most cases, they will still be too close together for the plants to develop fully, so before they become overcrowded, the surplus seedlings must be pulled out, leaving the others at the right distance apart, taking into account their ultimate height and spread, which is always printed on the packet.

The surplus seedlings can be transplanted into other positions, but they do not take kindly to disturbance, and will not do as well as those left *in situ*. And since seeds are relatively inexpensive, the usual practice is to throw them away.

Sowing time can be from the end of February to the end of May, depending on when the ground is in fit condition, or when it becomes vacant, following spring-flowering bulbs, such as tulips, daffodils, etc. In any event, the surface must be dry, especially where the sowing operation involves treading on the ground.

If the site is an isolated little patch between other plants, a pinch of seeds just thinly scattered over the area and lightly raked over is enough.

If several patches of different varieties are going together, lightly mark the area shapes with the point of a stick, or with a line of sand or lime. Sow each patch separately, taking into account their possibly different heights, then rake over.

If sowing in rows for cutting, draw shallow grooves (drills) ½ in deep and 24 in apart if there is more than one row. Fill in with the back of the rake after sowing, and lightly rake over.

The depth of sowing depends on the seed size. The smallest need hardly any covering at all; the largest, such as sweet peas and *Lavatera*, can be pushed in separately about 1 in deep.

In all cases they are quick to come through, taking only a few days, and at this stage, a few slug pellets around and among them is a good insurance.

There is often a temptation to water the surface after sowing with a fine rose on the can; but this almost invariably does more harm than good, because it causes a hard 'cap' to form on the surface, so preventing the seedlings from breaking through. Watering is, in fact, rarely needed, but if the ground is really dry, it is better to wet it first, twelve hours or so *before* sowing.

Autumn sowing
Some hardy annuals, as mentioned previously, give earlier, bigger and better flowers when sown in late summer and

Seeds of eschscholtzias are best sown in autumn.

autumn. They are always at risk, while small, in their semi-dormant state through the winter, the risk being less in the warmer southern half of the country and in gardens with light, well-drained soil.

A certain amount of luck, too, is needed with the weather. It must be kind enough, in the weeks immediately after sowing, for them to grow sufficiently big to withstand the worst effects of winter, but not too kind, or they will become soft and lush, and more liable to winter damage.

The end of August or early September is the best bet, but it must be accepted that success is something of a gamble in many places.

The practice is nearly always confined to varieties suitable for cutting, in order to guarantee good length strong stems. For this reason autumn sowings are generally made in rows for easy flower gathering, and in some cases so that they can be conveniently covered with cloches in winter. The use of cloches considerably shortens the odds against winter losses.

Sweet peas are often given the special treatment of being sown in pots or pans in a cold frame in October, or in a warm greenhouse in January or February. They are then set out, when 4–6 in high in April. Alternatively, and more simply, they can be bought at that time as plants.

Either way, they make a strong and extensive root system, and take careful transplanting in their stride.

Cultivation of hardy annuals

Hardy annuals other than sweet peas need very little care and cultivation while growing. Once they are through the ground and have been thinned out, they can look after themselves better than most. They must, of course, be kept free of weeds, and regular picking off of the dying flowers will give a slightly longer flowering time. Some varieties will benefit from having inconspicuous twiggy sticks pushed into the ground between them to keep them upright.

Taller varieties growing in rows for cutting, where straight stems are essential, can best be supported by pushing in canes at intervals along both sides of the rows and fastening strings alongside, perhaps at two different heights.

Slugs are their worst enemy, and sparrows sometimes find the seedlings attractive. Blackfly, too, tend to collect on nasturtiums. Otherwise very little bothers them.

To sum up – hardy annuals have a comparatively short flowering life, but are quick and easy to grow in almost any soil and situation, providing an inexpensive and quick show of colour and interest in the garden.

4. HALF-HARDY ANNUALS (CATEGORY ONE)

The familiar boxes of 'bedding plants' that appear like magic in April, May and June, often in the most unlikely retail outlets, are either genuine half-hardy annuals or plants to be treated as such (see earlier reference). The 'half' in their title indicates that the first part of their lives is spent as small seedlings and growing plants, in a greenhouse and/or cold frame. This is because they are very liable to be damaged by frosts that may occur during their early growing period from February to early May. The cold tolerance of these plants may differ slightly as will the frost patterns in different parts of the country, but as a rule, they must be kept protected until around the middle of May.

They flower over a longer period than the hardy annuals, offer a more varied choice, and are a reliable means of providing masses of colour in the garden from late June through perhaps to early October. In parks and public gardens they are freely used to create spectacular mass effects of intricate patterns and colour schemes.

Yet they are also flowers for the small garden, in beds and borders around front lawns, in

A spectacular bed and border display of half-hardy annuals.

tubs and urns on patios and backyards, and in window boxes, pots, troughs and hanging baskets. They include the petunias, marigolds, alyssum, lobelia, stocks, asters and many other favourites. And although they are unmatched for brilliant, varied colour, much of their value in the garden undoubtedly derives from the way they 'fit in' with other things.

When the frosts of autumn blacken and finish them off, they are cleared out and thrown away, just at the right time (the *only* time), for replanting those beds and borders, tubs and window boxes, with bulbs, wallflowers, polyanthus, forget-me-nots, etc. that are to stand through the winter and put on their most welcome show in the spring. And, very conveniently again, the latter finish in late May, just in time for the new HHA bedders to go in.

This continuous twice-a-year cycle of bedding for spring and bedding for summer will give the maximum amount of flower it is possible to grow in this country from one patch of ground in one year. But it involves considerable work. Seeds have to be bought, plants have to be raised, and beds have to be dug and replanted twice a year at specific times.

It is for this reason, and to save expense, that gardens are increasingly being planted with more permanent and less work-intensive subjects. Roses, flowering shrubs, heathers, conifers and perennial plants are in great demand, and container growing of these, plus their easy availability in garden centres, has

encouraged this trend.

Not that HHAs are ever likely to disappear from the gardening scene. In fact, seedsmen and raisers of new varieties have been stimulated by the competition into breeding even bigger, better and healthier flowers.

The cost of doing it yourself

The seeds of most HHAs have to be sown early under glass, preferably in warm conditions. This can be costly, for it entails a greenhouse and cold frame (although these of course, are used for other crops as well), compost, containers and, most expensive of all, heating.

In general, you should reckon that a temperature of 60°F (16°C) will be needed to germinate the seeds. Since not much space is needed for this, a small electric propagator is a very useful asset. A start will have to be made at the latest by mid-March or mid-February for the slower subjects and very important, a reasonably big area will have to be set aside to accommodate seedlings that are growing into plants, and kept at no lower than 45°F (7°C) until the middle or possibly the end of April.

Seedsmen always have something new to offer – new varieties, colours, shapes and sizes – and these are always expensive. The price of the packets may be the same, but the number of seeds inside them can vary greatly. This applies particularly to the modern strains of what are known as F1 hybrid seeds. The production of these involves very strict control of the parent plants, including growing them

22

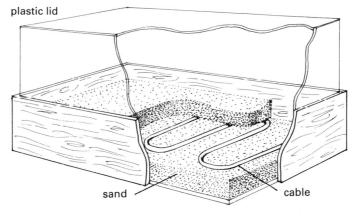

plastic lid

sand — cable

A home-made propagator with bottom heat supplied by an electric soil-warming cable buried in the sand.

in complete isolation, and often the very time-consuming job of cross-fertilising them by hand. And this is always reflected in their high price. In their favour, however, is the fact that they do 'deliver the goods', for they possess extra vigour and have qualities such as uniformity, lasting power, disease and weather resistance, built into them by their strict breeding.

Other factors that affect the price of seeds are in nature's hands. Some varieties are not so free in producing seeds as others and are always in short supply; and some need warm, dry weather to produce seeds in quantity, and have to be grown abroad in sunnier climes.

Quality is also reflected in the price. Considerable time and labour is required to keep the parent seed crops examined and rogued to make sure the offspring are true to type and name. The seeds have to be cleaned thoroughly after harvesting, packaged and finally distri-

buted. The best firms guarantee replacements if, for any reason, seeds fail. So varying prices are not always just matters of the seed firm's whim.

Rules for sowing

Plants of half-hardy annuals have to be ready to set out in the garden from about the third week in May until the middle of June. And to get the very best from them in the following summer, they must be at their very best during these two or three weeks. If they are too small, they take longer to come into flower and may never get to their best; if they are too big, and start flowering before they are planted out, they take a check in growth and may not fully recover.

The seed-sowing date, then, is all-important. And, because of the different growing speeds of different subjects, this usually has to be staggered. The classic example is that of the 'terrible twins' alyssum and lobelia,

23

favourite edging plants for years, planted alternately in white and blue around beds and borders. To get these two at the same time, and in just the right state for planting out together, lobelia has to be sown in February, alyssum in the second half of March six weeks or more between them.

There is no need, of course, to choose specific days when this or that should be sown, but when growing a mixed bag, it is well worth sorting the seeds out into two or even three sowing groups – around early February, early March and towards the end of March.

Once planted out, HHAs are not difficult and will grow and flower reliably in most cases. But the period from sowing to planting is more demanding, particularly the first two or three weeks. This is the time when many are lost, through varying temperatures, over- and under-watering, over-exposure to strong sunshine, and even rough handling. Some kinds, especially the early starters, can be tricky, even for the experienced grower.

Providing heat

The first thing to ensure is that the temperature needed to get good seed germination – 60°F (16°C) – can be maintained whatever the weather outside. Heat rising from below is best, and this can be most economically provided by the 'greenhouse within a greenhouse' method, namely a small area, covered with glass or polythene, over the source of heat. It can be achieved by a small electric propagator, or,

better still, by a soil-warming cable laid in a bed of sand on the greenhouse staging, surrounded by a frame of wood, with 9 in or so sides, and covered with polythene. The special electric cables are quite safe, and the whole apparatus can be temporary or permanent, as required. Boxes and pans placed on this bed are in ideal conditions for good seed germination.

Compost and containers

The sowing compost is very important as well. It must be clean and disease-free, light and open in structure, well drained yet capable of holding moisture.

Making up such a mixture is not easy, and as the proprietary seed composts sold in convenient plastic bags fulfil all these conditions, and only a comparatively small quantity is needed, for seed sowing the cost should be regarded as money well spent. When larger quantities are needed later for the 'pricking out' stage, it may be a different story.

The containers – boxes, pots or pans – must also be clean. Otherwise they may be the means of introducing the dreaded 'damping off' disease, whereby tiny seedlings are attacked by a fungus which rots the stems at soil level and causes complete collapse, often through the whole container.

The compost must not be pressed down too hard, but needs to be consistently firm all over. The aim is to get a perfectly flat and level surface, a half inch or so below the top of the container on which to sow. The best way is first to fill up loosely, scrape across the top to remove surplus. Then firm it all over with the fingertips, paying strict attention to the corners, top up again to the container rim level, then press down evenly and flat with the bottom of a pot or something similar.

Ideally, the compost should be moist enough before sowing to require no more water until the seedlings are through. And although this may not be possible for the slower germinating seeds, it is always worth soaking the filled boxes or pans, either by thoroughly spraying over the top with a fine rose on the can, or better still, holding each one half-submerged in water until the top is moist, and leaving to drain for 24 hours. Never try to water immediately after sowing; always do it well before.

Sprinkle the seeds on the surface, spreading them thinly, and for the smallest of seeds, which are invisible on the soil, just press them gently and carefully into the surface with no soil covering at all. For slightly larger seeds, cover lightly with compost 'riddled' on through a fine kitchen sieve. Larger, easily visible seeds, such as French marigolds, need covering with about a quarter inch of compost.

Cover each box, pot or pan individually with a piece of glass and sheet of newspaper, and stand them in position over the source of heat.

Stages in seed sowing: (a) Firming down compost. (b) Watering the compost. (c) Sieving soil to cover seeds. (d) Covering tray with glass and newspaper.

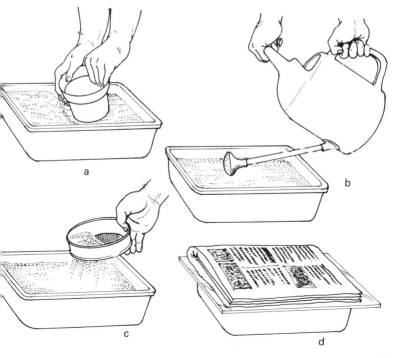

a

b

c

d

Getting them through

The time taken for the seeds to germinate and show through the surface varies according to the subject. Some may take only three or four days, others may take the same number of weeks. An indication of germinating time often appears on the package. The information is important so that the newspaper and later the glass can be removed in time. More failures occur at this stage than at any other.

As the time approaches, the containers should be examined once or even twice a day. Each container should be picked up and inspected crossways, as the smallest seedlings will be virtually invisible looking down from above; and if they are *not* seen at this time, and the paper not taken off, they draw up like a fine spider's web and invariably collapse when eventually they *are* recognised and uncovered. This regular examination is vital. Miss the seedlings for only a day, and the whole effort may be a waste of time and money. Larger seedlings are of course, quite easy to spot, but their treatment at this time must be just the same.

Other dangers at this stage are of exposing them too quickly and suddenly to full and direct light, and of the compost surface becoming dry. For a couple of days, the paper and glass can be propped up gently to shade them, gradually giving them more and more light, until after a week or so they are in full light without being exposed to full, strong sunlight.

The move out of the propagator should be done gradually so that the seedlings are not too much affected by the change of temperature. Once two leaves have been made, they will be better with less heat: 45°-50°F (7°-10°C) is about right, but for the first week or so, it may be worth taking them out of the propagator in the day, and putting them back at night. So much depends on the weather outside at this time of year.

Very great care must be exercised should they need watering at this stage. If they dry out completely, it is fatal; if they are kept too wet, it just could be fatal. So if there is any doubt, water them – *not* by spraying overhead, *always* by soaking from below, using the method already described.

'Pricking out' and 'hardening off'

Seedlings need more space as they grow into plants, and so, before they become overcrowded and start to interfere with one another's progress, they must be transplanted or 'pricked out' into other containers, to give them more room.

If they are left bunched together too long, they quickly draw up thin and weak, and are in danger of rotting because no air can pass between them. Pricking out can be done as soon as they can be safely handled.

Now is the time, of course, that they start to take up much more room in the greenhouse, and an estimate has to be made of the numbers of each subject wanted. It is no good pricking out too many boxes of one type and finding there is no room for others. Remember they still have to be kept inside and space is usually limited, temporary shelves are very useful in a greenhouse at this stage.

The compost for these second containers can be a no-soil potting compost, a John Innes No. 1 soil compost, or a home-made mixture of soil, peat and sand, plus fertiliser.

As there is still a possibility of introducing disease, everything must remain clean, and the proprietary ready-made sterile composts are generally the safest bet, although, of course, the most expensive. They are also weed-free.

Fill the boxes with moistened compost, press down as for seed sowing, top up again, level off and flatten the surface.

Standard-sized trays will take about 36 plants in six rows of six, although this can be slightly adjusted either way for different sized subjects.

In general, the more space they are given, the better the plants will be, but spacing as a rule has to be a compromise between the numbers needed and the room available. Careful handling is essential, picking up each seedling by a leaf, rather than by the stem.

Certain subjects are difficult to grow well in boxes, seedling geraniums, salvias and bedding dahlias, for instance, and these are all the better for being potted up separately into 2½-3 in pots. The advantage of this is that they can be moved farther apart as they grow. Furthermore, if bad weather delays planting them out, they will stand longer without spoiling.

The initial watering, after pricking out or potting, is best done overhead with a fine rose on the can, giving enough to soak and settle them in. And for the first two or three days, they should be stood out of direct sunlight. When they begin to perk up, after a day or two, full light is essential right away, or they will become thin and drawn.

The process of transferring

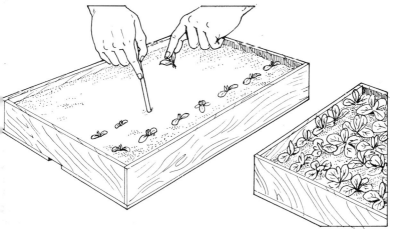

Pricking out seedlings, a delicate but essential operation.

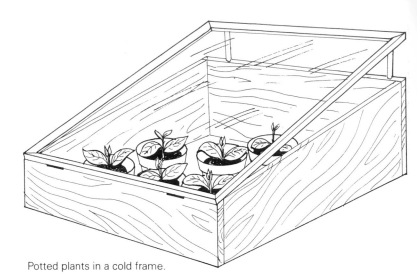

Potted plants in a cold frame.

them from inside to outside is known as 'hardening off'. It has to be a gradual business, and to act as the half-way house, a cold-frame is needed. A well-made frame is always an asset, but it can be nothing more than four walls about 12 in high of almost any material, covered with a sheet of polythene.

This move will be sometime in April, earlier or later according to when the seeds were sown, and of course, according to the season. This offers a good opportunity to hold each box half submerged in water for a few seconds. If the overhead sprinklings in the greenhouse have not soaked right through, this base watering makes a spectacular difference.

For the first week in the frame, the top cover should be kept on or, at most, propped up only an inch or two. After that, more and more air should be admitted, until they can be left completely exposed throughout the day, except in very heavy rain, and re-

covered at night. In fact, if a night frost is forecast, it may be necessary to extra cover them with an old carpet or something similar, not forgetting, of course, to take it off again the next morning. By mid-May, they should be ready for planting out.

HHA's without a greenhouse

All these instructions may suggest that raising HHAs is a complicated business. It isn't as bad as it sounds, but a lot has to happen in a comparatively short time, and it doesn't pay to make many mistakes.

As in all gardening, however, some variations in procedure are possible. You can, for instance, use an airing cupboard to provide the 60°F (16°C) needed to get the seeds started. But *only* to get them started. They *must* be moved as soon as they start coming through, and although a windowsill may house them for a day or two, good seedlings cannot be raised here, because light coming from one side only is not enough.

Similarly, some of the easier, quicker plants such as alyssum and French marigolds can be sown late – say in April – on a windowsill, and by pricking them out in early May they can be set straight outside at that time in a sheltered spot, and covered with polythene for a few nights. There are some risks using these methods, and the resulting plants may not be ready to plant out until late June; but it *can* be done, and if successful, even late plants can be very useful.

Buying ready-grown plants

Plants can always be bought. Garden centres and other outlets are full of them from around the middle of April until the end of June, and the quality can vary from good to very bad. These plants are often offered for sale too early for them to be taken home and planted outside. Mid-May is the earliest planting-out time, *not* before. If boxes of plants are bought before that, the correct thing to do is to keep them as they are, well sheltered against a wall or fence, regularly watered, and possibly covered at night.

Many commercial growers are also guilty of pricking out too many plants per container. The spacing is a clue. If they seem overcrowded, don't buy. If they look pale and drawn, don't buy either, as they will probably have been forced and hurried along in too much heat, and not hardened off properly. Such plants suffer badly when set out.

Look for strong, good-coloured, well-spaced plants.

The big disadvantage of buying plants, however good they are, is that as far as varieties and colours are concerned, you have to take what is on offer. Of the hundreds of different subjects and varieties to be found in a catalogue, or in a seed-rack, only comparatively few are sold as plants. Commercial growers are not too keen on growing dozens of different varieties. It tends to complicate their operations, so they concentrate on growing a few of the most popular. And they may well be the most popular simply because the buyers and growers aren't aware that anything different exists.

Planting out half-hardy annuals

If plants are to take the place of spring bedders – bulbs, wallflowers, polyanthus, etc – there is quite a bit to do. The finished plants have to be dug up, the ground must be cleared of the inevitable weeds, forked over – never dug up in large lumps at this time of the year, possibly watered, and some 'Growmore' or similar fertiliser raked into the surface at 2-4 oz per square yard (55–110 g per m^2). Very wet or very hot dry weather can delay the work, but a big effort has to be made to get planting done, at the latest, by the second week in June.

If plants are going into previously prepared vacant ground, there are about three weeks in May–June when planting can be done, and it need not be rushed in unsuitable weather.

If planting formal beds, work

out in advance the numbers required, the patterns and colour schemes, so that when conditions are right, there need be no delay.

Distances apart vary from about 9 in to 15 in or even 18 in depending on what can be expected from the plants, and erring by planting on the close side, rather than the other way. Nothing looks worse than fully grown plants that have not met their neighbours and covered intervening ground.

Never tread the ground more than can be helped. Have plants within easy reach, if possible, rather than keep walking backwards and forwards. Pressures in different places on the soil will result in different growth. A plank or small board to tread on is often useful.

If planting near a grass edge that has to be kept mown, try to estimate for the fully grown plants to reach the edge without overflowing and smothering it. Err by leaving more of a gap than not enough. On the other hand, if it is along the edge of a concrete or stone path, plant so that the edge will be disguised as the plants grow.

If planting a bed in the centre of a lawn, put the outside row of edging plants in first. If you do it, as may seem more sensible, by starting in the middle and working outwards, the last row rarely falls just where you want it.

Use a trowel for planting, not a dibber, firming each one in with the fingers, and water each one individually, however moist the ground is, because this will bring the soil and the roots into close contact and ensure a good start.

A few scattered slug pellets might be a good insurance, and the finishing touch should be added by lightly pushing a dutch hoe between the plants to leave an attractive, fresh-looking surface.

Effective lawn bedding.

30

Half-hardy annuals are, of course, perfect plants for any kind of container, window boxes, tubs, baskets, etc. Like anything else growing in these restricted conditions, however, they depend on being watered well, whenever they need it. The passing shower or two of rain is seldom sufficient. Rain will be prevented by the leaves from reaching the surface or sometimes, especially in a window box, will not touch the plants at all. In any case, water evaporates much more quickly from a container than from the garden. Regular watering, with a once-a-week liquid food in the water, is essential to keep things going.

5. Hardy Biennials (Category One)

Biennials, which grow one year and flower the next, are among nature's losers in this country, because they have to live through a winter as only partly developed plants.

Many of them are not tough enough to be completely reliable. Consequently they play only a comparatively limited role in the flower garden. As mentioned, most of those that are grown are really perennials – not, as a rule, very reliable perennials – 'grown as biennials'.

Wallflowers are a typical example. An odd wallflower plant will sometimes, if conditions are just right, live for several years. But to keep up a continuous reliable supply of them, we have to sow seeds afresh every year. This puts them, and a few others like them, alongside the annuals in our Category One.

Another flaw in the make-up of biennials in our climate is that by the time they have flowered and produced their seeds – in general by July and August – it is

Wallflower seeds are best sown afresh every year.

too late to sow that seed for flowering for the following year. It has time, of course, to germinate and grow, as is often seen when sweet williams or forget-me-nots shed their seed and produce hundreds of small seedlings round a parent plant; but not many of them live through. They are not big and strong enough to stand the winter, and almost inevitably fall victim to slugs and bad weather.

To raise successful plants, seeds from the previous year have to be sown in April, May or June, so that they have the whole of the summer and autumn to grow into good plants. Then by October, when they naturally stop growing, they are big enough to stand a fair chance of survival. Even here there is a danger. If we grow plants too big, they may also be soft and lush, and therefore more vulnerable to winter's low temperatures.

No wonder biennials are something of a poor relation.

Sowing and growing hardy biennials

Biennials, if they are to develop into sizeable plants, need plenty of room for growing, and space usually has to be found outside the flower garden proper. For instance, the seedlings of wallflowers and forget-me-nots, two of the best spring bedders, need to be set out 9 in or so apart, in rows 12 in apart. The vegetable garden is often the best place for them, sometimes the *only* place. They can, for example, in July, go into the ground from which early potatoes have been dug and cleared, occupying it until October.

Biennials are generally sown out in the open when the ground is warm in April, May and June. A small nursery bed needs raking down finely and the seeds go in short V-drills around half an inch deep. Apply a trickle of water all along the bottom of the drill before sowing. Keep a special look-out for slugs and sparrows.

Wallflowers, sweet williams, forget-me-nots, *Bellis* (daisies), foxgloves, Canterbury bells, stocks, pansies, Iceland poppies and hollyhocks are all quite easy to grow.

Polyanthus can be treated as biennials too. In fact, they will give their best flowers in the first year after sowing, and for this reason are often sown afresh every year, and the old plants thrown away after flowering. Grown this way they need a slightly earlier start than most of the others, mainly because they are slow in the early stages. They are best sown in pans or boxes in a warm greenhouse in February or March, pricked out into boxes like half-hardy annuals, and planted out around July in nursery rows to grow on.

It cannot be emphasised too strongly that all plants grown as biennials have to be given plenty of space at this growing-on stage. They *must* develop into good plants *before* being set into final positions in the autumn. It cannot be done in any hole or corner of the garden. They must be treated as important plants if good results are wanted, and given a good open position in reasonable ground, with space to expand. A drop of water to each individual plant when transplanted will get them quickly established, and all through the summer they must be kept hoed and free from smothering weeds.

Buying plants

Plants can be bought ready to set out in September–October or in February–March. The autumn plants are the better buy because biennials planted in spring come into flower before they have a good root hold, and do not have much chance of doing well.

Even autumn plants should be examined carefully to see that they are good specimens. Wallflowers, for instance, often sold tied up in bundles, may be single stemmed plants pulled straight up from the seed rows. As such they are of little use, producing only a single stem of flowers.

Transplanted specimens, on the other hand, will have bushed out, and though they will be more expensive, nothing like so many are needed to cover a given area; having done all their growing in the past summer, they will stay as they are through the winter and produce a good bush of flowers in the spring.

Planting in final positions

An effort must always be made to get biennials finally planted out while there is still some warmth in the ground. Early October gives them the chance to get established, and every week's delay after that makes it more difficult for them as bad weather develops.

Although the ground may be moist, watering them in indi-

Pansies, although perennials, flower best if treated as biennials.

dually always helps to get them away to a good start.

Their flowering period extends, according to subject, from late April to July. So only those that flower in April and May, fit into twice-a-year bedding schemes with the summer flowering half-hardy annuals.

Wallflowers, deservedly popular for their colour and sweet

scent, can be cleared by the end of May, fitting in very well with the early June planting of beds for summer. Forget-me-nots flower at the same time, and these two, interplanted with daffodils or May-flowering tulips, or even on their own, are the classic spring bedders. So, too, are polyanthus and pansies, and, to some extent, daisies. Most of the other subjects flower too late to continue with summer bedding schemes.

Sweet williams flower throughout June and July, finishing too late to clear and plant anything else in their place. So do stocks, Iceland poppies, foxgloves and Canterbury bells. They are best used as fillers between perennial plants in borders rather than in beds, though sweet williams can be grown in a separate row as they make superb cut flowers.

6. HARDY PERENNIALS (CATEGORY TWO)

The popular definition of a hardy flowering perennial is a plant that will live indefinitely, and produce its flowers without attention every year. But 'indefinitely' is not strictly accurate. Michaelmas daisies, admittedly, seem to go on for ever; but *Aquilegia* (columbines) definitely do not. And 'without attention' is a bit of wishful thinking. Whereas a clump of *Solidago* (golden rod) will live and thrive for years without anyone as much as lifting a finger, others, like delphiniums, need slug protection, shoot thinning, staking, tying, feeding, mulching, dead-

heading and dividing to keep them at their best.

All the same, hardy perennials are the easiest, most accommodating and most reliable flowers we can grow. And although there are, and always will be, kinds and varieties that have specific likes and dislikes – dry or wet places, sunshine or shade, heavy or light soils – most of them are quite happy in almost any site and normal situation and will live for several years.

They do, in fact, give an impression of permanence even in a newly created garden; and this is a great part of their value. Well chosen and placed trees and shrubs are the ultimate signs of an established layout, but in some cases these may be *too* big, or possibly a little *too* permanent. This is where the HPs plug the gap. Nor do they all disappear each winter.

The term 'herbaceous' perennial is applied to those whose top growth dies and is cut off at the end of each season; but there are some perennials with tops that live unharmed from one year to another. Irises, pinks, heucheras, bergonias and the grey-leaved *Anaphalis* are just a few that always show. And although they may not have any great decorative value in the middle of winter, they will, carefully placed, be better to look at than bare frozen ground.

Growing positions

The most important factor affecting the performance of the majority of hardy perennials is the amount of light or shade in which they are expected to grow. Peony in dense shade, for instance, might produce a good crop of leaves, but there will be few, if any, flower buds, and these on stems too drawn up and thin to support them. Even those plants recommended for shady spots will usually produce sturdier flowering stems in the open.

Although they are hardy perennials, delphiniums respond best when given plenty of attention

There is a difference, however, between dense shade beneath trees, where very few things will grow, and the dappled shade thrown by a tree's branches. Many perennials appreciate the latter, and will flower longer when planted in positions out of the glare of the direct midday and mid-afternoon sunshine. *Dicentra spectabilis* (bleeding heart) is a good example of this.

At the same time, though, it has to be remembered that if the light only strikes them from one side, they will always grow towards that side, and they may have to be staked and tied accordingly. This can happen in the case of tall delphiniums set against a high wall, leaning towards the light.

Planting under or near trees also brings other dangers – for example, pests. Trees harbour aphids (greenfly) and the sticky deposits from these which drop on to plants and encourage the development on their leaves of the unsightly black growth known as sooty mould. Earwigs and various caterpillars will always be a problem, and even the drip of heavy rain (as from a brief summer thunderstorm) from trees on to flowers underneath may be enough to ruin them.

Another notable point to take into consideration is the difference between shade from trees and shade from walls or fences. Plants growing near trees, and especially underneath them, are in fierce competition for the available food and moisture. Tree roots take an immense amount of both these essentials from the soil, which quickly becomes poor and dry.

On the other hand, ground against a wall or fence can be too wet or too dry, depending on the direction of the prevailing wind and rain. The north-facing side of a wall is always wetter and several degrees cooler than the south side; and although the moisture difference between the east and west sides may not be so marked, the west will always be warmer, and plants in general are more favoured.

The effectiveness of HPs as flowering plants, however, is controlled by the amount of light they receive. The majority of them can take temperature differences in their stride, many will grow in damp or dry soils, but almost all must have full light for at least part of the day to produce their maximum amount of flower on good stems.

This is one of the main reasons for development in recent years of the hardy perennial island bed. The older idea of a herbaceous border against a background wall or fence, although convenient and effective if well done, always produced – at least in the back part – plants drawn up by the half light, too tall and too weak to stand up for themselves, necessitating time-consuming staking and tying. Island beds in an open site without such influences produce plants of natural height and spread, and save much labour. With this in mind, new varieties of many plants have been bred with shorter and tougher stems, but with no loss of flower. These are the hardy perennials of today. The old favourites, such as lupins and delphiniums, always needed support to keep them upright. Now they, and many others, come as short strong-stemmed plants that need no staking or tying at all.

The modern way with HPs in the small modern labour-saving garden, is to use them as middlemen in a mixed situation. Shrubs are carefully chosen and placed as ever-present winter and summer attractions. Hardy perennials of different heights and forms are placed between them, not only for their own decorative value, but to cut down on the labour and cost of filling the smaller gaps with spring bulbs and summer annuals, both colourful, but comparatively expensive fly-by-night beauties.

This system, once established, works well, giving a succession of interest in form, leaf and flower throughout the year.

Specimen plants

Although a shrub, preferably shapely and evergreen, is the ideal plant to grow as a specimen, a favourite flowering HP is not out of the question. Admirers of *Kniphofia* (red hot poker), for instance, might think them attractive enough to plant in a small bed to themselves. The very striking *Acanthus* is often used this way, as is the tall, creamy *Aruncus* (goat's beard).

Some HPs in fact, are used more as specimens than in any other way. *Cortaderia* (pampas grass) is perfect to grow in complete isolation. So, too, is *Agapanthus* (African lily), often

seen as a tub plant on the patio. Unlike a specimen conifer or evergreen shrub, however, there are inevitably times when even the best of HPs are no great ornament, so this has to be taken into account when one is to be planted alone. Its flowers or shape must be good enough to warrant it being given this conspicuous treatment.

Ground cover

Hardy perennials can be used as weed smotherers in two different ways. Some, like epimediums, tolmeias and tiarellas, take over the ground with their spreading roots and need to be positioned with great care to prevent them becoming invasive and a nuisance if mixed with less vigorous plants. Others prevent the growth of weeds by blocking out the light with their large leaves, and hostas and bergenias are perfect examples of these.

It must be said, however, that these kinds of plants make ideal summer homes for slugs and snails, which hide in and among them during the day, and venture out on their damaging food expeditions at night. A few slug pellets are advisable.

Preparing the soil

If plants are expected to grow well in one position for several years, as is the case with hardy perennials, it is only common sense to prepare the planting site well. It is a common mistake to think that because many of them are easy-going, almost anything will do. There is a big difference, however, between merely existing, as they will in poor soil, and flourishing, as they will if trouble is taken to enrich the ground.

A good soil structure, brought about by digging the top 9 in and breaking up the bottom 9 in with a fork, at the same time generously working in manure, compost, peat or leaf-mould – collectively known as humus – will pay dividends. Roots are encouraged to grow and spread into these materials, and a good root system is essential to create and maintain maximum growth.

It is hardly possible in practical terms to overdo this initial ground treatment. On light, hungry soils, it gives body, weight and moisture-holding properties. And on heavy soils, exactly the same materials and treatment prevent it settling into a solid mass that roots can hardly penetrate.

This added humus may in itself contain very little actual plant food. Different materials possess varied amounts of nutrients. Peat, for instance, has none at all, while good farmyard manure may be very rich. Their main function, however, is as a ground conditioner. Humus, whatever it is, will give soil a good structure, and that is of primary importance.

The classic way of adding the nutrients for long-standing subjects is to dig in at planting time a slow-acting fertiliser. Bonemeal or hoof and horn mixture at 4-6 oz per square yard (110-170 g per m^2), mixed in with the top spit, will go on releasing food all through the vital first year after planting, and both are suitable for all kinds of plants.

These principles of ground preparation are the same whether for a long herbaceous border, a small group of plants or just one single plant. But in the last instance, do not merely dig out a small hole big enough to take the roots and no more. On heavy clay soils this can be a death-trap, where the plant will drown from water standing there as if in a sump. The minimum preparation for any one plant should be 18 in square, with double that size for bigger plants.

The ideal is to get this preparation done well in advance of planting, giving the ground time to settle naturally. A large border would be best dug in the autumn for spring planting, or dug in the spring for autumn planting, using the interval to plan where the different subjects are going, and marking the exact spots with canes. The same applies to a single plant, although if absolutely necessary, preparation and planting can be done at the same time provided the ground is broken up well and the plants well firmed in.

Planting

Many hardy perennials are nowadays sold growing in containers, and since there is no root disturbance, these can be set out at almost any time of the year. Dwarf subjects, in particular, can be set out even in full flower. But this cannot be recommended for the taller growers, which are almost sure to be blown around by wind and will have difficulty in anchoring themselves. In any case, with container plants, large or small, set out in late spring or

40

at any time through the summer, there is always a danger of the root ball drying out independently of the surrounding soil; and if there is a period of drought at this time it means that they will have a struggle to become established, and may even die.

Throughout the first summer, then, it is essential that container-grown plants should be soaked several times after planting – and not by light overhead spraying, as with a garden sprinkler, but individually soaked so that the root ball is thoroughly penetrated. Showers of rain at this time can be very deceiving. They may perhaps keep the surface moist, but do very little towards soaking the ground. It takes a lot of summer rain to have any real effect.

Planting time for dug-up-and-divided bare-rooted subjects can be either in autumn (October–early November), or in spring (March–April.) A few, such as scabious and *Aster amellus*, prefer the spring move, but in general October, when most plants are becoming dormant and the soil is still warm, is a good all-round planting month.

In the heavier, difficult-to-work clay soils, it is a distinct advantage to make up a planting mixture a few days in advance, consisting of half peat or leafmould, and half sand or soil. As the plants are set in the hole, work in a handful or two, in immediate contact with the roots. This makes it easier for them to get a hold, and ensures a good start.

Roots, if free, should be spread out in the planting hole,

Fine soil should be worked around the root ball of a container plant.

Firm the plant in with the foot.

The hole for bare-rooted plants must be deep enough for the roots to hang straight down.

41

and even if from a container, it will pay lightly to tease a few away from the solid ball, encouraging them out into the surrounding soil.

It is difficult to generalise about planting depths, but they should never be shallower than they were previously. The same depth or very slightly deeper will not be far wrong. Firm the soil all round, and apply a pint or so of water immediately after planting to each plant, to bring the soil into sufficiently close contact with the roots.

A few slug pellets around is always a good insurance, particularly in the case of subjects with fleshy shoots, such as delphiniums. Bad attacks by this pest in the early spring can sometimes spell the sudden end of any new plant.

The spacing and arrangement of plants are also matters of individual decision, taking into account the height, spread and colours of the chosen subjects. No matter what the size of the patch, however, a group of three or five of one kind, set close enough together to mingle with one another when in flower, is generally better than single dotted plants. And if there is a back and a front to the site, the taller things, of course, go at the back.

Choice

The great range of hardy perennials makes it good policy and sense to consider well the possibilities before making a final choice. Height, spread, vigour, colours and flowering time, preferences for wet and dry positions, for shade and for sunshine, should all be taken into account.

Even among such commonly grown subjects as Michaelmas daisies and golden rod, for example, varieties are available that range in height from 6 in to 6 ft. Delphiniums and lupins now come, if so required, in short, stumpy varieties that need no staking or tying, even in the most exposed situations. The common *Achillea*, so often seen as lanky plants with flat yellow heads of flower, can now be had as Galaxy hybrids, short front-of-the-border plants, in white, pink, purple and red as well as yellow. Different leaf colours, too, are always attractive. Even the well-known grey, woolly *Stachys lanata* (lamb's ears) has a new relation, just as soft and woolly, but a pure gold instead of silver. And the common *Heuchera* can now be had in a dark purple-leaved form.

A keen eye kept on nurserymen's stock, new catalogues and other people's gardens, will often reveal new varieties, sometimes of old favourites with a surprising new look. And although just one small plant of some of these can be comparatively expensive, the beauty of most hardy perennials is that in a short time, and with very little trouble, more can be made of them.

Even so, this simple multiplication can be a dangerous feature. Plants that increase easily are easy to acquire from friends, relations and, among the gardening fraternity, even from complete strangers. Such offerings, though difficult to refuse sometimes, can often be bettered. A good variety is just as easy to grow as a bad one. With HPs it pays to be choosy and to look around.

Flowering time is perhaps the most influential factor. The earliest and latest subject may not be the most spectacular, but away from summer, even the most modest display is very welcome. Who wouldn't, for example, find a corner for a Christmas rose, or a clump of the pink or purple *Helleborus orientalis*? And what better to light up a dull corner in March and April than the easy-going golden daisies of *Doronicum* (leopard's bane)? In summer, of course, there is no trouble to create a show and in the autumn

Michaelmas daisies and chrysanthemums will go on into November in a good season.

Propagation by division
Whether or not we want to increase our stock of hardy perennials, there comes a time when we need to know how to propagate them. This is because most of them, sooner or later, become less attractive as they grow older, or need replacing as they exhaust the ground in which they are growing. Paeonies, for instance, will thrive in the same spot for years, but fibrous mat-rooted subjects like Michaelmas daisies, etc. should be split up every three or four years to keep them young and vigorous.

The Lenten rose, *Helleborus orientalis,* is an early flowering perennial.

Two forks may be used to divide large clumps. Use the outside parts and reject the central portion.

Two forks may be used to divide large clumps. Use the outside parts and reject the central portion.

This division of old roots is the easiest of all propagating methods. In many cases it can be done either in spring or autumn, although some things such as scabious and catmint are fussy, and prefer to be moved just after they have started growing in the spring. An approximate rule is that spring flowerers are divided in the autumn and summer flowerers in the spring.

After carefully digging up the old plants, select vigorous young shoots with roots attached from around the outside for replanting. The old centre portion is generally worn out and not worth keeping.

If the idea is to rejuvenate a group of perennials and replant them in the same ground, it is a good idea to dig the old plants up

in the autumn, and set them temporarily somewhere else. The ground can then be thoroughly dug and manured, removing any weeds, and the selected new pieces replanted in spring in the well-settled ground. The rooted pieces can be set singly or, to cover a larger area, in threes or fives a few inches apart, to be treated as one plant.

Where the purpose of propagation is to increase stock, shoots can often be taken off without disturbing the original plant and interfering with its growth and flowering. Use an old knife or trowel to sever rooted pieces carefully, and put these in pots to be kept and grown on until they are needed, perhaps the following year.

Propagation from bare cuttings

To raise new plants from subjects that are difficult or impossible to divide, shoots can be taken off as bare cuttings in spring and summer, and put in to make an entirely new root system. They do this best in a closed humid atmosphere under glass; setting them in pots or boxes in a closed cold frame is ideal. A cloche can be used if the ends are closed up, or a single cutting can be rooted under a jam jar in the open ground.

Where cuttings are particularly plentiful, as, for instance, with pinks, it is even worth trying some in the open ground without covering. Choose a moist, shady spot, and set them in an inch or so deep in a V-trench lined with a half-peat, half-sand mixture. A daily overhead spray is needed to keep them fresh. In general, shoots 2–3 in long should be selected, either pulled from the parent plant at that size, or trimmed to it with a sharp knife after taking off the bottom leaves. Dipping the ends in hormone rooting powder or liquid will assist rooting, but shade, moisture, a light mixture to set them in, and patience are the essentials.

Propagation from root cuttings

Some HPs, among them oriental poppies and *Anchusa* have thick fleshy roots with dormant growth buds on them. These types can be propagated from root cuttings, a useful method when a lot of new plants are required.

Take a piece of root in the early spring, cut into inch-long pieces, and set the thickest, end up, in a box of seed compost with the top just level with the surface. Cover this with a half-inch layer of coarse sand, and keep moist and shaded. They soon start to grow,

and when they have made a few leaves, they can be potted separately, and grown on until big enough to plant.

Bearded irises are one of the few HPs best propagated in midsummer. When a clump of their tuber-like rhizomes has become overcrowded, they should be dug up when flowering has finished in July, and the outside ends cut off with a sharp knife to give half-rhizomes with leaves and some roots. These are then replanted at the same depth as previously and the worn-out centre rhizomes thrown away.

Plants propagated either by division or cuttings are said to have been raised vegetatively. They will always be exactly the same as the parent plant they came from, and in some cases, this is the only way to be absolutely sure of true reproduction.

A divided iris, with roots, section of rhizome and leaves.

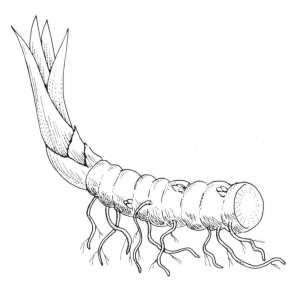

Lupins and delphiniums, for instance, can easily be raised from seeds, but the seedlings are likely to be variable, different from the parents in height, habit or colour. It is only by vegetative propagation that new plants of these and many other subjects can be produced, exactly the same in every respect.

Growing from seed

Although in theory all subjects should make seeds from which new plants can be raised, some do not, particularly in our climate, and some are sterile because they are hybrids, the result of cross-breeding. Many of those that do produce seeds, do not pass on their own characteristics entirely. The very feature for which they are grown may not appear in their offspring.

In practice, therefore, it is not advisable to grow certain perennials from seed. Nor, of course, is it necessary, seeing that vegetative propagation is reliable, quick and, in most cases, easy.

Reliable seeds of some subjects, however, can be produced by seed firms who make carefully controlled crosses, or by growing parent plants in complete isolation, often abroad in warmer climates. Even with these there may be small variations from plant to plant, generally in colour or shade of colour. These may be quite acceptable, however, as in alstroemerias and aquilegias, where good colour mixtures are the norm. It is variations in height and habit that are most likely to cause problems.

If you do decide to gather and sow seeds more or less randomly, remember that it may take a long time, perhaps several years, to grow plants to flowering size, that plants and flowers may be variable, and that valuable time and space will be taken up before these variations will be known, and the best plants selected to grow on.

Sowing hardy perennial seeds

There is one remarkable difference in the way seeds of HPs germinate. Some are quite happy to be harvested and kept for several years, if necessary, before sowing, still retaining their ability to grow when the right conditions come along; others lose their power to grow, their viability, very quickly, and give best results when sown almost immediately after harvesting.

Typical of the latter is the whole *Primula* family. Hundreds of self-sown seedlings can often be found coming up in the autumn, around a cowslip or a polyanthus (both members of the family), just where they have dropped only a week or two before. Yet if this same seed had been gathered and kept packeted for sowing in spring, only a low percentage would have germinated. Their viability would have been lost.

Some of the long-keeping seeds have to experience winter temperatures and be frozen before they will germinate well. Hellebores and *Hemerocallis* (day lily) for example, are best sown in the autumn in pots or pans, and left outside through the winter to germinate when the weather changes in spring.

The majority of HPs, how ever, can be sown from March until June. The aim must be to produce plants in that first summer, big and strong enough to come unharmed through their first winter, and sowing time should be geared to this.

Notoriously slow growers are best sown in March in a warm greenhouse. Quicker growers can be sown in a cold house or frame in April or May, or even outside in June.

The method of sowing is the same as for half-hardy annuals (see page 22). A good seed compost, well moistened in pots, pans or boxes, thin sowing, and very fine covering if seeds are small, with a sheet of glass and paper on top.

Seedlings are pricked out in boxes when big enough to handle, or, more likely with HPs, potted up individually. Then they are gradually introduced to outside conditions as they grow, and planted in their permanent positions when convenient, either in the autumn or the following spring. Some, such as delphiniums, will even produce the odd flower in their first autumn, but the small plants will grow bigger and better if this is not allowed to develop and it is pinched off as soon as seen.

7. HALF-HARDY PERENNIALS (CATEGORY THREE)

Half-hardy perennials have to be something a bit special to be grown outside as garden flowers. To keep them through the winter, they must be dug up and kept safe inside, then planted out again in the following spring. They are more work and a lot more trouble to keep alive than hardy perennials. Consequently, they are mainly grown by enthusiasts, who not only take this extra work in their stride, but also have the luxury of a heated greenhouse in which to keep them.

Tender subjects such as heliotropes, lantanas and penstemons were at one time widely grown in parks and public gardens to create exotic and lavish bedding schemes. Now, with the rising cost of labour and heating, they are fast disappearing as common plants.

Even that popular mainstay of park bedding schemes, the geranium, is now mostly grown anew every year from freshly sown F1 hybrid seed rather than from cuttings taken from the old plants and kept through the winter. A classic example of half-hardy perennials being grown as half-hardy annuals. The specialised production of F1 hybrid seeds has made this possible.

It is no coincidence that three of the most popular hobby plants of the gardening enthusiast, namely geraniums – the established named varieties grown from cuttings, not those raised from seed – dahlias and chrysanthemums, are all half-hardy perennials. Plants such as these keep green fingers occupied all the year round. The very fact that they thrive on constant care and attention, protecting, propa-

Named varieties of chrysanthemums are grown from cuttings.

gating, potting and planting, is just what enthusiasts are looking for.

There is no danger of these three particular HHPs disappearing from the garden scene. In fact, there are thriving National Societies that promote and encourage their growing in every possible way, not least by sponsoring exhibitions and competitions at both local and national level.

Apart from the well-known tuberous rooted dahlias and begonias, the old plants of HHPs are rarely kept for replanting. In most cases, cuttings are taken either in late summer or autumn and grown on steadily inside during the winter. Alternatively, as with chrysanthemums, cuttings are taken in the spring from roots that have been protected through the bad weather. These, with their entirely new set of roots, make new young plants with better flowering potential than would be possible from old plants. In fact, old plants of certain subjects are not good movers, and taking cuttings is the best way of keeping them for another year.

8. BULBS, CORMS AND TUBERS
(CATEGORY FOUR)

The value of spring-flowering bulbs in the garden is obvious even to the most inexperienced gardener. Daffodils, tulips, hyacinths, etc. are among the best known and easiest of plants to grow. Anyone, even a child, can plant a new bulb in the autumn, and be almost certain that it will produce a flower in the spring.

New bulbs, in fact, bought from a good supplier, are among the best bets in gardening. The commercial producer for his own good is bound to give them the right treatment during the preceding season, and this means that the flower, or at least the flower bud, is already formed inside each bulb, and that only something very drastic can stop it forcing its way out when the time comes.

Corms and tubers are slightly different. They are all classed as 'bulbous-rooted', but unlike bulbs, the bulbous part is purely a food supply, and the flower is not formed inside during the previous year. With the same ready-made source of food to draw on, however, they have almost the same flower-producing potential as bulbs.

Crocuses are the best known of the spring-flowering corms, and quite the easiest to grow. If left undisturbed in a spot that suits them, they will go on flowering and increasing every year, what-

ever the weather. This easy-going habit makes them, along with many varieties of daffodils, classic subjects for planting in situations where they will be left entirely alone – naturalising, as it is called – to provide a welcome trouble-free show each spring.

Orchards, rockeries, grassy banks and tree-shaded places where very little else will grow can all be made attractive with no more trouble or expense than the initial buying and planting.

A golden rule

The one rule that should at all times be observed with bulbs is that the leaves must not be cut off, but allowed to develop fully, then die down naturally, a process that takes several weeks after flowering has finished. The temptation to 'tidy up' when the flowers have gone, particularly when subjects are planted in grass that needs cutting (lawns,

Massed daffodils produce an attractive woodland effect in a garden setting.

51

orchards, etc.) has to be avoided. The leaves are the food factory of the plant, and if they are cut off prematurely, the bulb suffers, and the next year's flowers are affected, indeed there may not be any. Eight to ten weeks after flowering is the earliest the leaves can be safely removed. By then the life in them will have returned to the plant and their job is done.

This principle applies to all bulbs in every part of the garden. In a flower border, the clever gardener will disguise this untidy period by setting them among leafy plants that as they grow will hide the dying bulb foliage. Paeonies and hostas are good examples. Their large leaves, expanding quickly in early summer, will effectively cover the dying-back bulbs with no detriment to either plant. Many other herbaceous border plants and small deciduous shrubs can be used in this way.

Bulbs in formal bedding
Daffodils, tulips and hyacinths are, of course, magnificent for formal spring bedding, either massed alone, or interplanted with wallflowers, forget-me-nots, daisies or pansies. In these situations, because the bulbs have to be completely cleared after flowering for summer bedding plants to go in, a different technique must be used. The principle of the leaf nutrients returning to the bulb has to be maintained, even though they have to be moved; so they must be dug up carefully with the leaves intact, and immediately replanted.

The 'dying-down' site can be in any spare bit of ground, the complete plants being laid down quite close together at an angle in a shallow V-trench, and the bulbs then covered with soil. A good watering will settle the soil round them, and help minimise the disturbance. After six weeks or so they can be dug up, cleaned off and stored dry for replanting in October. This digging-up operation can be made easier if the bulbs are buried in a plastic slatted basket, or even set with a piece of wire or plastic netting underneath them. This keeps them together when lifting for cleaning, and there is no fear of leaving any behind.

Even with such careful treatment, however, the effect of this enforced and untimely move of bulbs used for formal bedding will be seen in next year's flowers. They are never quite so good in the second year. Flower quality will be down, and some may not flower at all. They are best planted in informal clumps in borders, or naturalised in uncultivated ground where they will give quite an acceptable overall display. And in subsequent years, if the position suits them, they should improve and multiply.

For a good reliable spring bedding display, it is always best to use new bulbs. In practice, however, this is an expensive business, particularly if large numbers are required.

The ground for bulbs
The fertility of the ground makes very little difference to the flowering performance of the bulb in

the first season after planting. A good bulb will always, barring accidents, produce a good flower. But to ensure that it goes on producing good flowers in subsequent years, it must produce good leaves, and to do this, it appreciates a bit of help from the ground. Peat, leaf-mould or compost, worked well in before planting, will encourage good roots, the basis of all good plants, and a sprinkle of bone-meal at planting time and immediately after flowering will provide all the food needed.

Mother and daughter bulbs

The manner in which bulbs multiply means that even under the best conditions, some, left undisturbed in any clump, will not flower in any given year. This is because they will not be big enough; and there are two distinct reasons for this. Firstly, the new young bulbs, called daughter bulbs, that form naturally around the older bulbs, known as mother bulbs, take more than one year to reach flowering size; and there are bound to be *some* daughter bulbs. Secondly, if bulbs are overcrowded, as they surely will be in time if not moved, there will not be enough food to keep them all doing well. Some are bound to suffer.

The difference can be detected, with a keen eye, in the vigour of the clump. If it is healthy and spreading, daughter bulbs are being made, and until they are overcrowding each other, they are best left to their own devices. If the clump is not expanding, and the flowers are progressively smaller every year, as well as fewer in number, it is generally from overcrowding and resultant starvation.

Dwarf tulips provide masses of colour in March and April.

In this case, they are best dug up in July or August, and separated. If they are going back in the same place, once the soil is replenished, the biggest bulbs can be replanted. The smaller ones can be planted in a spot where immediate flowering is not important.

Spreading the spring-flowering season

Daffodils and tulips alone, in their many varieties, will provide colour throughout the spring-flowering season. The earliest daffodils, typified by such dainty gems as 'February Gold' and 'Tête-à-Tête', can be guaranteed to flower annually in early March, sometimes in February. And there are many varieties, large and small trumpeted, double, single, multi-flowered, in white, cream, pink and red, as well as in all the glorious yellow shades, that will carry on the show well into May. Similarly, there are early dwarf tulips in magnificently rich colours, some even with striped leaves, such as 'Red Riding Hood', that flower reliably in March. Many flower in April, some, like 'Toronto', with several flowers to each stem. And the large May-flowering varieties, lily-flowered, parrot-flowered, 'Triumph', 'Rembrandt' and the well-known Darwin varieties, come in an astonishing range of colours and combinations of colour. They are among the most noble and stately flowers in any garden.

The height to which a variety will grow is given in most lists and catalogues. It remains constant under most growing conditions, except possibly in the shade; here the stems are likely to be a bit longer – drawn up by lack of light – and possibly a bit weaker as well.

It may not be of great importance in a large garden, but there are varieties both of daffodils and tulips, particularly the latter, that are too tall for some situations. For pockets in a rockery, for instance, the dainty dwarf early daffodils are perfect. And for a tub or window-box, the dwarf April-flowering tulips are superb. The wrong variety can look ridiculous. Height and site must always be considered together.

Hyacinths

The cost of hyacinth bulbs makes them expensive to be used on a large scale. But a dozen or so in a tub or urn or in a window-box will make a very colourful and fragrant feature, and they are particularly long-lasting.

In the garden, hyacinths are often the yearly plantings-out of bulbs that have been grown in bowls indoors. They may not flower after the first year of forcing, but in subsequent years they will produce a splash or two of sometimes forgotten colour, though never quite so good as when the bulbs are brand new.

Crocuses

Crocuses are inexpensive enough to plant in quantity. They do, in fact, need to be massed to be effective, and can provide the first real drifts of spring colour. Even a mere dozen bulbs are better planted close together in a clump than spread thinly in a dozen different places.

Crown imperials are distinctive additions to the spring border.

The earliest to flower, *Crocus thomasinianus* and *C. chrysanthus*, will sometimes show in January, but are at their best in February. The well known Large Dutch are the most spectacular, with very big white, blue and yellow flowers in March. They all like sunshine, and if they take to a spot will seed themselves and spread freely.

Miscellaneous bulbs

A number of other bulbs and corms that flower in the spring are generally listed as miscellaneous bulbs, and many are ideal subjects to plant and forget. Anemones, *Chionodoxa* (glory of the snow), *Eranthis* (winter aconite), *Erythronium* (dog's tooth violet), *Iris reticulata*, *Muscari* (grape hyacinths), scillas and, of course, snowdrops, are among the best known. They are mostly dwarf, easy-to-grow subjects, coming up and flowering regularly in February, March and April, and multiplying freely where the soil is well drained.

Fritillaria (crown imperial) are in a class of their own among these bulbs. They are plants for positions where they can be left undisturbed for several years as specimens. The yellow or red hanging bell flowers come on 3 ft high stems that grow quickly in April, and if they do well they produce more stems and more flowers each year. They can, however, be temperamental, and refuse to flower in some years. Even so, the stems and leaves are decorative in themselves, and a mulch of manure over the spot, when they have died down, will sometimes help the flower-building process.

The large bulbs look like peeled potatoes, and are unhappy out of the ground. They are only on sale for a short period, quite unlike other spring bulbs, and a good supplier keeps them buried in peat or sawdust prior to sale, something to look for when buying. A handful of sand under each bulb, when planted, encourages a good root system, and the tender pale green shoots which appear very early must be protected from slug and snail damage with slug pellets. The 'foxy' smell is sometimes considered a disadvantage, countered perhaps by the fact that it is supposed to keep mice out of the garden.

Bulbous-rooted summer flowers
Dahlias, begonias, gladioli and iris are among the most popular summer flowers that come from corms, tubers or rhizomes. But there are many lesser known species that will grace the garden in succession from June until the frosts.

Some of these are not hardy; the begonias and dahlias, for instance, have to be lifted and stored in frost-free places for the winter. Others are not so tender and, particularly in the warmer parts of the country, can be left in the ground and protected with a covering of leaves or peat a few inches thick; *Gladiolus byzan-*

tinus is a good example. And among many that can be left in the ground all winter with perfect safety are the large and varied family of lilies, montbretias, crocosmias, alliums, alstroemerias, camassias and many more. These will multiply if left undisturbed, though a danger is that their position may be forgotten in the winter and new shoots may be damaged by hoeing, etc. as they come through in the spring. For this reason it is always advisable to mark the spots where they are planted.

Begonias, dahlias and gladioli are much grown by amateur gardeners for exhibition. Various involved techniques of propagating, feeding and protecting them from weather damage are used to grow them without any blemish, and to their full potential, but they are also in great demand for ordinary garden decoration, where only the minimum of cultivation and attention is needed. Dahlias, gladioli and alstroemerias are especially good cut flowers, while begonias and *Agapanthus* are perfect in tubs and other outdoor containers.

Planting time for most of them is from March to May, according to subject. Broadly speaking, they are more responsive to good soil, good conditions and good cultivation than their spring-flowering counterparts.

The bulbous summer-flowering gladioli are ideal for outdoor display and cutting.

57

9. SELECTED LIST OF HARDY ANNUALS, HALF-HARDY ANNUALS AND HARDY BIENNIALS

ACROCLINIUM HA

Daisy-like flowers, mainly white and shades of pink, with strawy petals. Good for cutting and drying. Sow in April-May where they are to grow, and thin to 4-6 in apart. Any soil, sunny position. Height 15 in. July-August flowering.

AGERATUM HHA

Best known as a blue bedding plant, but there are also pink and white varieties, all around 6-9 in tall. There is also a taller 18 in variety, good for cutting. Long-lasting flowers, from July to October. Sow in warmth February-March. Plant out 9 in apart late May. All soils.

ALYSSUM HA or HHA

Most popular grown as HHA for dwarf white edging round larger bedding plants. Pink and purple varieties are also available. Sweet smell, but too 'powdery' for some. Height 3-6 in. Can be sown as HA in growing positions, rockeries, between crazy paving etc. in April-May, or in cold greenhouse or frame in March-April, or as HHA in warmth in February. Plant out late May, 9 in apart. Note. *Alyssum saxatile* is the yellow perennial alyssum.

Ageratum is a popular, long-flowering bedding plant.

AMARANTHUS HA or HHA

The 2-3 ft tall, long red-tasseled variety, known as Love-lies-Bleeding, can be grown as HA sown outside in flowering positions in April-May, or as HHA, sown in warmth in March, and planting out 2 ft apart in June. A green-tasseled variety is useful for flower arranging. There are also several varieties grown for their coloured leaves. Useful in beds or borders as 'dot' plants. Likes sunny positions.

ANCHUSA HA

Best variety is 'Blue Angel'. Masses of blue forget-me-not flowers on 9 in high plants. Sow in April where they are to flower, and thin to 9 in apart. Can also be sown in September to stand the winter. Flowering July-September. Note. *Anchusa*

azurea is the tall perennial species.

February, pinch out tips to make bushy plants, and plant out in May. Plants will sometimes live through the winter.

ANTIRRHINUM
Perennial, grown as HHA

Old-fashioned 'snapdragons' but also now with varieties that have open-ended tubular flowers. Many distinct varieties of different heights from 9 in to 3 ft, in distinct colours, bicolours, or mixtures. Good for mass bedding or on rockeries or in borders. Long-lasting if seed heads are cut off regularly. Sow in warmth in

ARCTOTIS HHA

Single 'daisy' flowers in pastel and brilliant yellow orange and red colours, on 18 in stems. Good for cutting. Flowers close at night. Must have sunny growing position, and need twiggy supports to keep them upright. Sow in warmth in February-March, plant out in early June 18 in apart. Any well drained soil.

A representative colour range of *Aster sinensis*.

ASTER HHA

Popular single, double and anemone centred long-lasting flowers in almost all colours, distinct or in mixtures. Dwarf and medium height varieties for beds, 6-12 in. Taller varieties for cutting, up to 30 in. Later to flower than many HHAs, but good from August-October. Suffer from disease known as aster wilt. When this is known to be present in the soil, it is best not to grow asters. Sow in warmth in March, in cold house in April, or outside in May. Best in well-drained soil in open sunny site. Note. Michaelmas daisies are perennial asters.

BEGONIAS (Fibrous Rooted) Perennial, grown as HHA

Bushy plants with small white, pink or red flowers in great profusion, and glossy green, red or bronze leaves. Attractive over a long period, and useful for any situation, from massed bedding to hanging baskets. Can be dug up and potted before frosts for winter flowering. Best in good soil. Very small seeds, not easy to raise. Sow in warmth 70°F (21°C), January-February, taking great care until pricking out stage. Plant early June.

CALCEOLARIA (Outdoor) Perennial, grown as HHA

Once grown only from cuttings, but new varieties will flower quickly from seed. Bright yellow

Calceolaria rugosa.

'pouch' flowers on branching plants about 12 in high. Brilliant in masses and long-lasting. Small seeds. Treat as bedding begonias (see above).

CALENDULA Pot Marigold HA

Easy to grow. Rake seeds into surface wherever needed and thin seedlings to 9-12 in apart. Cream, yellow and orange flowers of different petal formations according to variety. Height 1-2 ft. Sow in March for summer flowering, or in September to stand winter and flower earlier. Best in poor soil.

CANDYTUFT   HA

Easy to grow. Sow as marigolds (see above). Thin to 6 in apart. Neat compact plants 9 in high in mixtures of pink, lavender, and white. 'Red Flash' is a distinct red variety, and 'Giant Hyacinth-Flowered' a 15 in high white variety. Good in masses or for edging, but finishes flowering in August. Sow in March or September. Any soil.

CANTERBURY BELLS   HB

'Old-fashioned' border flowers in pinks, whites and blues. Height 18-30 in according to variety. Sow seeds outside in ½ in deep drills in May-June. Transplant seedlings 12 in apart in nursery bed. Plant in flowering positions 18-24 in apart in October. Protect from slugs. Flowering May-July. Well drained soil for final positions. Can be grown as specimens in pots.

CHEIRANTHUS
Siberian Wallflower   HB

Flower later than ordinary wallflowers, (June-July) so not suited for beds that are to be cleared for summer bedding. Brilliant fluorescent flowers in distinct yellow and orange varieties. Good in masses. Sow and plant as Canterbury bells (see above). Height 12-15 in spacing 12 in. Best in limed soils.

CHRYSANTHEMUM   HA

Quite distinct from perennial varieties. 'Daisy' flowers in mixtures of bright colours, many with rings of contrasting colours. Height 12-24 in. Good for cutting, July-October. Sow in groups or rows outside, ½ in deep where they are to flower, and thin seedlings to 12 in apart.

CLARKIA   HA

Easy to grow. Spikes of flowers generally in pinks, whites and purples 12-24 in high according to variety. Grow in patches or rows. Good for cutting. Rake in seeds during April where they are to flower, and thin to 9-12 in apart. Taller varieties may need twiggy stakes in windy positions. Open sunny site. June-September.

CLEOME Spider Flower
HHA

Unusual plant that quickly grows to 3-4 ft high. Branches out and carries clusters of curious flowers with long stamens. White, pink and purple, long-lasting and useful as 'dot' or border plants. Ordinary soil. Sow in warmth in March. Plant out 18 in apart in late May.

CONVOLVULUS   HA

Related to common bindweed, but dies at end of the season. *C. major* is a climber reaching 8-10 ft. *C. minor* is dwarf and bushy,

12 in high. Trumpet flowers in blue, pink and white, June-August. Sow where they are to flower in March-April. Sunny position. Poor soil.

COREOPSIS HA

This annual is sometimes known as *Calliopsis*. Mostly yellow flowers on plants 1-2 ft high. Suitable for cutting. Best in patches in sunny positions. Sow where to flower in April. Thin to 12 in apart.

CORNFLOWER HA

Height ranges from 1-3 ft according to variety. Mostly blue flowers, but pink, purple and white also available. Good for cutting. Sow in rows or patches where they are to flower, March-May, or in September to flower early the following season. Any soil. Open position. Taller varieties may need support.

COSMEA HHA

Most common varieties are 3-4 ft tall, on slender stems with feathery foliage, and have white, pink or red single flowers. Newer varieties around 18 in with yellow and orange double flowers. All good for cutting, or to give long garden display July-October. Can be sown outside in May, or in warmth in March and planted out in late May. Ordinary soil.

DAHLIA (Bedding)
Perennial, grown as HHA

Dwarf dahlias from seed reach 1-2 ft, depending on variety. Mostly single flowers, but a few double varieties in almost any colour. Long flowering period July to October if dead flowers are picked off. Ordinary soil. Sow seeds in March in warmth, plant out early June. Makes tubers that can be dug up, stored and replanted the following year. Should not be confused with established named varieties.

DIANTHUS Annual Pinks and Carnations
Grown as HHA

Dwarf plants suitable for bedding, rockery, containers, etc., and taller plants for cutting, with many variations of flower form and colour, single and double. Flower over long period July-October. Height 6-24 in, according to variety. Sow February-March in warmth, plant out late May. Dislike acid soils.

DIGITALIS Foxglove HB

Good subjects for the dappled shade of trees. Tall varieties up to 5-6 ft. Shorter varieties 3 ft. Flowering June-August. Sow May-June, transplant seedlings to nursery rows, and plant in flowering positions in October. Leafy soil.

DIMORPHOTHECA HA

'Daisy' flowers in mixtures of 'art' colours, on low bushy plants up to 12 in. Good in patches in borders, rockeries, etc. Must have well drained soil and sunny position. Sow where to flower in March to May. Thin to 6-9 in apart.

ECHIUM HA

Upturned bell flowers, mainly blue, but also in mixtures of white, pink and purple. Bushy plants. Height 12 in. Long-lasting flowers June-October. Sow where to flower in March-May. Thin to 6-9 in.

ESCHSCHOLTZIA Californian Poppy HA or HB

Can be sown in April where to flower, but make bigger and better plants sown in flowering position in August-September. Silky-petalled large flowers with 'ferny' foliage, 6-12 in high. Can be had in single colours, orange or yellow, or in mixtures of 'art' shades. Must have full sun. Flowering June-September.

GAZANIA Perennial, grown as HHA

Very showy 'daisy' flowers with yellow and flame colours in many

Dimorphotheca is a useful low-growing rockery plant.

Geraniums, now available in many colours, flourish in sunny positions.

different combinations. Good for beds, borders, rockeries. Height 9-15 in. Must have well drained soil, and sunny positions. Flowers close on dull days and at night. Sow February-March in warmth, plant out early June. Flower July-October.

GERANIUM (F1 hybrids)
Perennial, grown as HHA

Expensive seeds, easy to raise, that will produce good flowering plants in July from sowings made in warmth January-March. Masses of flowers from July to frosts. Good in all situations except shade. Colours and bicolours according to variety, many with attractive zoned leaves. Grow seedlings on in pots, and plant out in early June. Plants can be kept inside through winter and cuttings taken for another year. Not to be confused with established named varieties.

GODETIA   HA

Easy to grow, and one of the best hardy annuals. Single, semi-double and double 'poppy' flowers on plants 12-24 in high according to variety. Generally in shades of pink mixed with white. Good for garden decoration and cutting. Taller varieties may need support. Sow March-April where to flower, or in September for earlier flowering. Thin to 6-9 in.

GYPSOPHILA   HA

Small white and pink flower in sprays, very suitable for cutting and using with sweet peas, etc. Height 18 in. Sow where to flower March-May, or September, and thin to 12 in apart. Flowering June-September. Dislikes acid soil. Note. *G. paniculata* is the perennial species.

HELICHRYSUM   HA or HHA

'Everlasting' flowers with strawy petals in many bright colours. New dwarf varieties, 12 in, good for bedding, taller varieties, up to 3 ft, good for cutting and

drying. Sow outside in April, or in warmth in February-March. Plant out in late May 12 incm) apart. Likes full sunshine. Any soil.

HELIOTROPE
Perennial, grown as HA

Used to be grown from cuttings of named varieties, but can be grown from seed. Violet-purple flat heads of flowers 15-18 in high. Good for bedding and sweet scented. Likes warm positions in full sunshine. Sow February-March in warmth. Plant out early June 12-15 in apart.

HOLLYHOCK   Perennial, best grown as HB

Well known tall plants 4-8 ft tall, with single or double flowers in many colours. Sow as Honesty (see below). Some varieties can be sown January-February in warmth for flowering in their first season. Growing positions must be carefully chosen, because of plant height.

HONESTY   HB

Purple and sometimes white flowers in June-July followed by flat silvery seed heads, prized for winter arrangements. Strong-growing plants 2-3 ft high. Sow outside in May-June in flowering positions, or in nursery row, and transplant in October for flowering the following year. Will grow in shade. Any soil.

A spectacular mixed display of long-flowering busy lizzies.

IMPATIENS Busy Lizzie
Perennial, grown as HHA

Modern F1 hybrid varieties are superb in beds, borders and all containers. Low growing 6-9 in spreading plants, massed with flowers in many dazzling colours and bicolours, that can be bought separately or as mixtures. Good in damp shady places but will grow anywhere except hot dry spots. Can be dug up before frosts, and potted for growing inside during winter. Sow March-April in warmth, plant out early June 9-12 in apart.

LARKSPUR HA

Good spikes for cutting, 1½-4ft, according to variety. Pink, lavender, violet and white flowers with feathery leaves. Sow seeds outside in flowering positions in March-April, or in September for early flowering. Tall varieties may need support. Flower June-August. Any soil.

LAVATERA Mallow HA

Big bushy plants, 2-4 ft covered with pink or white large single flowers July-October. Good for garden decoration where there is plenty of room, and excellent for cutting. Sow in March in flowering positions, or in September to flower earlier. Thin seedlings to 2 ft apart. Any soil.

LIMNANTHES Poached Egg Flower HA

Very good low-growing 6 in spreading plant, covered with yellow and white flowers and 'ferny' foliage. Good in patches at front of border, or on rockeries, etc. Flowering June-October. Sow in March in flowering positions, or in September for earlier flowers. Sunny position, any soil.

LOBELIA HHA

Well known as a blue 4 in high compact edging plant, but can also be had in white or crimson, or as a mixture. Trailing varieties for baskets, etc. are also available. Sow seeds in warmth January-March. Prick seedlings out in small groups rather than single plants, and plant out in late May-early June. Long lasting (June to September) in moist ground. Seeds small and need attention after sowing.

MARIGOLD HHA

African, French and Afro-French varieties are by now almost indistinguishable from one another, but they are all easily grown bedding plants for almost any situation. 6 in to 3 ft

high, according to variety, and mainly in yellow, orange and red. Single or double, they flower over a very long period (June to frosts). Sow in warmth March-April, plant out in early June. Best in sunshine.

MATRICARIA Grown as HHA

Bushy plants, 9 in high, covered with small white or yellow flowers. Useful in a mass or as edging. 'Chrysanthemum' leaves have pungent smell. Sow February-March in warmth. Plant out late May, any soil.

(Left) *Lobelia* 'Crystal Palace'.
(Above) French Marigold 'Beau Nash'.

hybrid varieties do well in full sunshine. Red, yellow and orange trumpet flowers with contrasting markings. Good in containers if kept well watered, and as pot plants. Height 6-12 in, according to variety. Sow in warmth March-April. Plant out late May 12 in apart.

MESEMBRYANTHEMUM Livingstone Daisy   HHA

Flat-growing spreading plants that must be in full sunshine to flower. 'Daisy' flowers in many bright colours and bicolours, good for dry walls, rockeries, etc. Flowers close at night and on dull days. Sow in warmth March-April. Plant 6-9 in apart during early June. Flowering June-September.

MIMULUS   Perennial, grown as HHA

Good bedding plants for shady damp places, although new F1

MYOSOTIS Forget-me-not HB

Well known blue carpeter for beds of tulips; also in pink, 9-12 in high, spreading to 12 in across. Sow outside in May-June; transplant to grow on in summer, and plant in final positions in October. Flowering April-May.

NASTURTIUM   HA

Very easy to grow trailing or bushy plants that thrive in poor soil. Useful for covering awkward banks, etc. and in containers and baskets. Mostly yellow,

69

orange and red flowers, appearing throughout season. Sow seeds in flowering positions in April-May. Will grow anywhere, but flower best in full sunshine.

NEMESIA HHA

Multi-coloured flowers appearing early in the season (June), but bushy plants can be trimmed over at the end of July to flower again in August-September. Best in mixtures, but can be had in blue alone, 9-12 in high. Sow March-April in warmth. Must be grown well in boxes to avoid premature flowering. Plant out in early June.

NICOTIANA Tobacco Plant HHA

Much-improved varieties now give good colour mixtures on dwarf plants 12 in high. Flowers face upwards, and stay open all day. Tall fragrant varieties, 3 ft, still available for garden decoration. Sow in warmth March-April. Plant out early June. Flowering June-October. Any soil or position.

NIGELLA Love in a Mist HA

Now in all colours, as well as the well known blue. Attractive feathery foliage and seed pods. Flowering July-August, 15-18 in high. Sow in patches in flowering positions in March-April or in September for earlier flowering.

Thin to 9 in apart. Any soil. Easy growing.

PANSY Perennial, grown as HHA or HB

Favourite long-flowering plants that come in all colours and combinations of colours. Good in beds, borders and all containers, particularly window-boxes and tubs. Need constant dead-heading to prolong flowering. Sow February-March in warmth and plant out in late May, or sow outside in drills in July-August, transplant into nursery bed to grow on, and into flowering positions in October. Some varieties will flower in winter during mild spells.

Nigella 'Miss Jekyll'.

PETUNIA   HHB

Long flowering plants for any situation. Bushy plants 9-12 in high with trumpet flowers in mixtures, or as separate colours. Single and double flowered varieties, grandiflora types with particularly large flowers. Especially useful in baskets, tubs, window-boxes, etc. in sunny positions. Sow February-March in warmth, plant out in early June.

RUDBECKIA   Grown as HHA

Long-lasting 'daisy' flowers in brilliant orange, yellow and mahogany red, separate or in mixture. 15-18 in high varieties good for bedding, 2-3 ft varieties good for borders and cutting. Sow during February-March in warmth, plant out in early June. Flowering August-October.

SALPIGLOSSIS   HHA

Exotic-looking trumpet flowers in all colours, veined with other colours. Must have warm sheltered positions to do well. 12-30 in high, according to variety. Taller kinds need some support. Sow February-March in warmth, plant out 12 in apart in early June. Flowering July-September. Good for cutting. Also make good pot plants.

SALVIA   HHA

Good bushy bedding plants with spikes of red flowers, 9-12 in high. Also available in pinks and purples. Must be grown well in early stages. Sow February-March, in warmth. Plants are best grown singly in 3 in pots rather than pricked out in boxes, pinching tip to induce bushiness. Plant out early June in good soil and water in. Flowering July-October.

STATICE   HHA

'Everlasting' flowers with papery sprays of flowers in many bright colours, very good for cutting and drying. Height 18-24 in. Sow in warmth February-March, plant out early June 12 in apart. Likes well-drained soil, and sunny position. Note. *Statice latifolium* is perennial.

STOCKS   HA, HHA and HB

Sow HA Night-scented and Virginian stocks in flowering positions in April. Sow HHA Ten-week stocks in warmth February-March and plant out late May. Sow HB Brompton stocks outside in June-July, and plant in flowering positions in October. Fragrant single and double flowers in pink, purple, blue and white. Suitable for bedding and cutting.

SWEET PEA   HA

Favourite sweet-scented flowers for cutting, but also good for garden decoration, flowering over a long period, June-September, if flowers are cut regularly. Many colours, separate or mixed. Dwarf varieties 18-36 in. Climbing varieties 6-8 ft need support. Can be sown in pots in cold frame in October, to plant out in March for early flowering and longest stems, or in warmth in February for April planting, or seed can be sown direct in flowering positions in April.

SWEET WILLIAM   HB

'Old fashioned' fragrant flowers with strong stems very good for cutting. Single colours or in mixtures. Dwarf edging varieties 6 in high, others 18 in. Sow outside in May, transplant 9 in apart to grow on, and plant in flowering positions in October. Must be good strong plants at planting time.

TAGETES   HHA

Bushy 9 in high plants of the French marigold family with the same pungent smell, covered with small single flowers in yellow and orange. Long flowering period, July-October. Good in masses or as edging for beds. Sow March in warmth, and plant out early June 12-15 in apart. Good in tubs, etc.

THUNBERGIA Black-Eyed Susan   HHA

Climber or trailer needing a warm sheltered spot in full sun. Good in hanging baskets or as pot plants. Single flowers in orange, yellow or white on plants that will climb 6-8 ft. Sow in warmth, March-April. Plant out in mid-June. Average soil.

VERBENA   Grown as HHA

Mainly low-growing 9-12 in spreading plants with heads of small flowers in many bright colours and bicolours. Good for bedding, edging or in containers. *V. venosa* is a taller upright-

Thunbergia alata.

Viscaria 'Rose Angel'.

Zinnia.

growing species, with purple flowers on 15 in stems. Sow in warmth February-March. Plant late May.

VISCARIA   HA

Easy to grow. Single flowers in red, blue, white and pink on 12 in high plants. Must be sown in masses to be effective. Flowering July-August. Sow March-May in flowering positions and thin to 4 in apart.

WALLFLOWER   HB

Excellent for spring beds and borders. Fragrant flowers in many colours, mixed or separate. 12-20 in high according to variety. Sow outside May-June,

transplant 9 in apart for summer. Must be grown well to make bushy plants for setting out in October 12-15 in apart. Mix well with daffodils, tulips, etc. and can be cleared in time for summer bedding. Siberian wallflowers need same treatment, but flower slightly later, and over a longer period.

ZINNIA   HA

Flowers of all colours on plants that vary according to variety from 9 in to 30 in high. Must have warm sunny position and are best in a warm season. Good for bedding and cutting. Flowering July-October. Sow during March-April in warmth and plant out early June. This plant needs good soil.

73

10. SELECTED LIST OF HARDY PERENNIALS

ACANTHUS Bear's Breeches
HP

An impressive long-lived plant that is best in an isolated position. Fleshy deep-growing roots make it drought resistant. Purple and white flower spikes 4 ft high July-October. Handsome decorative leaves. Any well drained soil. Cut down late autumn. Divide when necessary in October-November.

ACHILLEA HP

Long-lasting flat heads of flowers on plants of different heights 2-5 ft, according to variety. Mainly yellow; Galaxy hybrids are a new race with cream, white, pink and red flowers on 18 in stems. Easy to grow, sunny positions. Divide when necessary in spring or autumn.

AGAPANTHUS African Lily
HP

Not recommended for cold exposed positions. 2-3 ft stems spring from clumps of strap-like leaves, and carry heads of blue or white flowers July-September. Good tub plant and for cutting. Needs good soil, sunny positions and water in dry spells. Divide carefully April-May.

ALSTROEMERIA Peruvian Lily HP

Temperamental plants sometimes difficult to establish. Need light rich soil and sheltered position. *A. aurantica*, with lily-like stems of orange flowers, is easiest. Ligtu hybrids in several colours are shorter, 30 in. Excellent cut flowers. Dislike being disturbed. Sow seeds in spring and grow to planting size in pots.

ANAPHALIS HP

Silver-grey leafed plants with 18 in stems of ivory-white 'everlasting' flower heads, August-September. Make a spreading ground cover mat of leaves and stems, but are not too invasive. Grow anywhere. Divide easily in spring or autumn.

ANCHUSA HP

Bluest of blue flowers, June-August, on plants of different heights 3-5 ft, according to variety. Tend to die after 3-4 years, particularly in heavy soils. Cut down after flowering. Best propagated by taking cuttings of fleshy roots in winter.

ANEMONE Japanese Anemone HP

Late summer and autumn flowering, 2-4 ft high, according to variety. Mainly white or pink single long-lasting flowers with golden central 'boss'. Spreads steadily but dislikes being divided. Propagate from root cuttings in winter. Well drained soil. Sun or shade.

AQUILEGIA Columbine HP

Dainty but short-lived plants with 'ferny' leaves and wiry flower stems from 6-36 in high, according to variety. Modern hybrids in many colours and colour combinations. May-June. Any soil but like partial shade. Awkward to divide, but mixed colours are easily raised from seeds sown in spring or summer.

ARUNCUS Goat's Beard HP

Mainly large, tall plants for moist shady positions in large gardens. Plumes of creamy-white spiraea-like flowers 6 ft high June-July. Old plants may reach 6-8 ft across. Imposing in right situations. *A. kneffi* 24 in high variety. Cut down in autumn. Difficult to divide.

ASTER Michaelmas Daisy HP

A wide range of plants varying in height from 6 in to 6 ft. Mainly flowering August-October. *A.*

amellus is distinct with large flowers, mainly blue, around 24 in high. *A. nova-belgii* is the true Michaelmas with varieties to suit almost any situation. Divide easily in autumn or spring. Divide *A. amellus* only in spring.

ASTILBE False Spiraea HP

Must have moist soil, rich in peat, compost, etc., and does best in partial shade. Plumes of white, pink, purple or red long-lasting flowers, according to variety. Upright stems 1-3 ft, with attractive leaves often reddish-bronze in early stages. Divide in spring.

ASTRANTIA HP

Sprays of small 'everlasting' flowers, pink, white and red, June August. Good for cutting and drying. Spreading plant in most soils and partial shade. Easily divided in autumn or spring.

BERGENIA Elephant's Ears HP

Easy growing, with large, low-growing leathery leaves, and thick-stemmed 12-18 in high sprays of white, pink, red or purple flowers in March-April. Spreading evergreen ground cover, easily kept in check. Grow anywhere, even under trees once established. Divide in autumn.

BRUNNERA HP

Sprays of blue forget-me-not flowers on 18 in stems, rising in April-May from a clump of large leaves that go on growing all summer. A variegated form has cream and green leaves. Good in shady positions. Any soil. Divide autumn or spring.

CAMPANULA Bell Flower HP

A very varied family ranging from dwarf rockery plants to 3-5 ft high border plants. Star- or bell-shaped flowers, mainly blue but also pink and white in June-August. Good for cutting. Easy to grow. Sun or shade. Cut down in autumn. Divide autumn or spring.

CATANANCHE Cupid's Dart HP

Cornflower blue papery flowers on 2 ft stems, rising from clump of grassy leaves. Good for cutting and can be dried. June-September. Like sunny position, and good in dry well-drained soils. Tends to deteriorate after 3-4 years. Best from seeds sown in spring.

CENTRANTHUS Valerian HP

'Grow anywhere' plants thriving in poor soils. Pink, red or white heads of small flowers, June-October, on stems from 18-30 in. Often seen growing in walls.

CHRYSANTHEMUM Shasta Daisy HP

Easy-growing branch of a large family, mainly white flowers although a few varieties flushed yellow. Large single, anemone centred and double-flowered varieties. Good for cutting, 2-3 ft stems. New dwarf varieties 1 ft. Any soil. Divide in spring when necessary.

DELPHINIUM HP

Upright spikes mainly blue, but also white and pink flowers, from 24 in to 8 ft tall. Excellent for cutting and garden decoration. Named varieties propagated by cuttings or division in spring. Easily grown from seeds sown in summer. Tall varieties need support. Cut down after flowering. Good soil. Sunny positions.

DIANTHUS Pinks and Carnations HP

Very varied family. Border pinks and carnations have grassy grey leaves and fragrant flowers in all colours and bicolours on strong 15-24 in stems. Good for cutting. Old plants deteriorate, but are easily propagated from cuttings taken in summer. Like limy well-drained soil. Sunny positions.

DICENTRA Dutchman's Breeches HP

Attractive leafed plants with arching 2-3 ft stem carrying

curious flowers, red, pink or white in May-June. Easy to grow in any soil. Light shade. Divide carefully in early autumn after cutting down.

DORONICUM Leopard's Bane HP

One of the earliest perennials to flower April-May. Yellow 'daisy' flowers on stems 6 in to 3 ft according to variety. 'Spring Beauty' is double-flowered. Good for cutting. Any soil. Divide in spring or autumn.

ECHINACEA HP

Single cone-centred flowers, pink-purple on long 3-4 ft stems. Late flowering, July-October. Good for cutting. Need fertile soil, but grows easily in full sunshine. Cut down at end of season. Divide in spring if necessary.

ECHINOPS Globe Thistle HP

Strong-growing thistle-like plant 3-5 ft high, with round blue flower heads that can be dried for winter use. Best in full light, but will grow anywhere. Cut down at end of season. Divide in spring, or take root cuttings.

ERIGERON Flea Bane HP

Single and semi-double 'daisy' flowers, blue or pink, 12-24 in high. June-August.

ERYNGIUM Sea Holly HP

Spiny thistle-like plants with silvery leaves, blue stems and silver-blue flowers in sprays, July-September, 18-36 in high, according to variety. Excellent for flower arranging. Some with marbled leaves. Seeds itself freely. Well drained soil, full sun. Dislikes disturbance. Cut down autumn.

GAILLARDIA HP

Tend to die out in 3-4 years, particularly in heavy soil, but can be raised from seeds sown in spring, or by careful division in March. Brilliant red and yellow large 'daisy' flowers on rather floppy plants. Good for cutting. Dwarf varieties 12 in high, others 2-3 ft. Light soils. Sunny position.

GERANIUM Cranesbill HP

Hardy and not to be confused with 'bedding' geraniums. Dwarf spreading, or upright clumps massed with pink, purple or white flowers, 1-2 ft according to variety. Flowers well in shade. Easy to grow. Any soil. Divide if necessary autumn or spring. Cut down in autumn.

GEUM HP

'Mrs Bradshaw' (red) and 'Lady Stratheden' (yellow) are best varieties, but tend to die out after 2-3 years. Easily raised from seeds sown in spring to give plants the following year. Other small-flowered varieties, orange and red, live longer, and can be divided in autumn or spring. Any position.

GYPSOPHILA HP

Small-leaved plant, producing large spread of 3 ft high thin but strong stems carrying masses of white or pink small flowers. June-August. Excellent for cutting and mixing with sweet peas etc. Must have non-acid soil. Any situation. Dislikes disturbance. Double variety 'Bristol Fairy' is difficult to propagate, but single will grow from seeds sown in spring.

HELENIUM HP

Easy to grow plants, 3-5 ft high, according to variety. Cone-centred single flowers, bronze-red and yellow, on strong upright stems, good for cutting. Need dividing every 3-4 years to retain vigour. Any position. Cut down in autumn.

HELIANTHUS Sunflower HP

Single, anemone-centred, and double yellow flowers, according to variety, on strong wiry stems 4-6 ft high. July-September. Easy to grow but need dividing every 3-4 years to retain vigour. Any soil. Sunny position. Cut down in autumn.

HELIOPSIS HP

Related to *Helianthus*, but shorter 3-4 ft bushier plants. Golden yellow mainly double flowers in July-August. Long-lasting when cut. Divide only if necessary in autumn or spring. Any soil. Full sun. Cut down in autumn.

HELLEBORUS Christmas and Lenten Roses HP

Single flowers, white, pink and purple, 9-18 in high. Valuable because of their winter and early spring flowering time. *H. niger* is Christmas rose. *H. orientalis* is Lenten rose. *H. corsicus* has green flowers and distinctive leaves. Moist soil. Partial shade. Divide after flowering or grow from seed.

HEMEROCALLIS Day Lily HP

Much improved new hybrid varieties have many colours. Sprays of trumpet flowers on 1½-3 ft high stems, according to variety, rising from clump of rush-like leaves June-August. Likes rich soil and moist position. Easy to grow when established. Divide autumn or spring when necessary.

HEUCHERA HP

Dainty but strong stems carrying sprays of small flowers, mainly pink and red, 18-24 in high. May-June. Evergreen mat of leaves provide ground cover, but needs lifting and replanting young pieces every 3-4 years. Variety 'Palace Purple' has dark leaves and white flowers. Any soil. Sun or shade.

INCARVILLEA   HP

18-24 in stems appear in May before the leaves, carrying deep pink trumpet flowers May-June. Ferny leaves follow. Needs position marked to avoid hoe damage. Well-drained soil. Difficult to divide. Grows from seed.

INULA   HP

Large yellow 'daisy' flowers with fine cut petals, on plants from 12 in to 6 ft high, according to variety. June-September. Tallest varieties only for large gardens. Easy growing. Any soil. Divide autumn or spring. Cut down in autumn.

KNIPHOFIA Red Hot Poker HP

Now in white and yellow shades as well as red. Clumps of grass-like leaves with 2-5 ft high flower stems July-September. Deep-rooting and long-lasting in well-drained soil. Tying leaves into a cone and mulching for the winter gives crowns needed protection in coldest positions. Divide autumn or spring. Mixed colours can be grown from seed.

Helleborus orientalis.

LIATRIS   HP

18-36 in spikes of pink or purple fluffy flowers in July-September opening from the top downwards. Clumps of grassy leaves new each year. Moist but well-drained soil. Sun or shade. Remove flower spikes when faded. Divide in spring.

LIGULARIA   HP

Large plants for moist shady places only. Large ground-covering leaves and 3-4 ft high stems carrying sprays or spikes of yellow flowers. July-September. Cut down after flowering. Divide when necessary autumn or spring.

LIMONIUM Perennial Statice HP

Large 2-3 ft high sprays of 'everlasting' minute pink or blue flowers, springing from large leaves and tough rootstock. July-September. Excellent for cutting with sweet peas, etc. and good garden decoration. Any soil. Full sun. Dislikes disturbance or division. Propagated by root cuttings in winter, or seeds in spring.

LINUM Perennial Flax HP

Dainty but wiry plant 1-2 ft high with narrow leaves and single blue flowers, repeatedly produced June-August. Likes full sun, and well-drained soil. Short-lived but easily raised from seeds sown in spring. Often seeds itself.

LUPIN HP

Stately spikes of flowers in June-July in all colours. Quick to grow and sometimes short-lived. Basal cuttings taken in March will give plants the same as parent. Seeds sown in spring give mixtures of colours. Dwarf varieties 2 ft, others 3-4 ft. Dislike lime, manure and waterlogged soils. Cut flower spikes when faded.

LYSIMACHIA Yellow Loosestrife HP

Vigorous easy-growing plant that spreads underground, but can be easily contained. 30 in high spikes of yellow flowers June-

August. *L. clethroides* has white flowers. Any soil. Sun or shade. Best divided every 3-4 years in autumn or spring.

MECONOPSIS Himalayan and Welsh Poppies HP

Two very different plants. Welsh poppy has yellow single flowers 12 in high June-September. Himalayan is blue, larger flowers, 3-4 ft high. Short-lived plants, but Welsh seeds itself freely. Sow Himalayan in autumn or spring. Lime-free soils. Partial shade.

MONARDA Bergamot HP

Curious flowers, pink, red, and purple, on 2-3 ft stems June-September with scented leaves. Needs moist soil in sun or shade. Matted roots need dividing every 3-4 years to retain vigour.

OENOTHERA Evening Primrose HP

Large yellow single flowers June-September on plants varying from 6 in to 2-3 ft according to variety. Must have well-drained soil and full sun. Divide in spring, except for *O. missouriensis*, which must be raised from seed sown in spring.

PAEONY HP

Long-lived plants that resent disturbance, and often take a long time to get established. Many varieties of large single and double flowers in many colours on 2-4 ft stems. Like deep fertile soils and partial shade. Decorative leaves. Remove seed heads after flowering. Cut to ground in autumn.

PAPAVER Oriental Poppy
HP

Large pink to red flowers, single or double, around 3 ft high in May-June. Easy to grow. Full sun, well-drained soil. Cut whole plant down after flowering to get a new crop of attractive leaves. Divide in spring, or take root cuttings in winter.

PHLOX   HP

Large trusses of flowers in all colours except yellow, on strong 2-3 ft high stems, coming late in the season   July-October. Dislikes hot dry soils and positions, and flowers best in light shade. Suffers from root-eelworm which shrivels and distorts leaves. No cure. Propagate from healthy plants by dividing in spring, or take root cuttings in winter. Cut down at end of season.

PLATYCODON Balloon Flower   HP

Flower buds like balloons which open to single long-lasting flowers, June-September, 1-2 ft high. Mostly blue but pink and white varieties available. Disappears completely so planting spot must be marked. Well-drained soil. Sun or shade. Difficult to propagate.

Oriental poppies do best in full sun.

Platycodon grandiflorus var *mariesil.*

POLYGONATUM Solomon's Seal HP

Must have cool shady positions in moist soil. Arching stems, 2-3 ft high, carrying pendant white, green-tipped flowers. Matted spreading roots that divide easily in autumn or spring. Cut down in autumn.

PRIMULA HP

A wide range of plants that includes primroses, cowslips and polyanthus. Candelabra types have flowers in 'whorls' on 1-3 ft stems, according to variety. Many colours. Best in shady moist positions with peat, leaf-mould, etc. Divide after flowering or sow seed in spring.

PULMONARIA HP

Early flowering, March-May. Shade and moisture-loving plants, some with spotted leaves. Pink and blue flowers on 12 in stems. Divide in autumn or spring to keep vigorous.

PYRETHRUM HP

Long-stemmed and long-lasting 'daisy' flowers at a useful cutting time, May-June. Single, ane-mone-centred or double and white, pink or red, according to variety. Clumps of 'ferny' leaves. Best in light soils, but must have adequate moisture. Full sun. Divide immediately after flowering. Can be grown from seed.

SCABIOSA Scabious HP

A new variety, 'Blue Butterfly', flowers June-October. Blue 'pin-cushion' flowers on plants 12-18 in high. Larger-flowered varieties have long stems, good for cutting over long period. Blue, purple and creamy white.

Like well-drained soil with lime.
Divide only in April.

SIDALCEA   HP

Long-flowering plants with 2-4 ft
spikes like small hollyhocks,
June-August. Pink and red. Any
soil. Best in sun. Cut down after
flowering to encourage basal
growth. Divide in spring.

SOLIDAGO Golden Rod   HP

Yellow plumes of flowers July-
September, in various heights,
1-5 ft, according to variety. Easy
to grow in good soil. Sun or
shade. Cut down in autumn.
Divide in autumn or spring.

THALICTRUM   HP

Maidenhair fern-like leaves and
branching stems of small white,
pink or purple flowers 2-5 ft
high, according to variety. June-
September. Good for cutting.
Likes shade and a rich moist soil.
Divide when necessary in
autumn or spring, or sow seed in
spring.

TIARELLA Foam Flower   HP

Evergreen   ground-covering
plant for shady places. Spreads
quickly in leafy acid soils. Foamy
creamy white flowers on 9-12 in
stems in May-June. Divide when
necessary autumn or spring.

TRADESCANTIA Spiderwort HP

Long-flowering 'grow anywhere'
plant, slightly untidy, with
'rushy' leaves and blue, white or
pink flowers, according to
variety, on 2 ft fleshy stems,
June-September. Any soil. Sun
or shade. Divide autumn or
spring.

TROLLIUS Globe Flower   HP

Large 'buttercup' flowers, cream,
gold and orange in May-June,
according to variety. Must have
rich moist soils. Good for pool
sides. 18-24 in, good for cutting.
Sun or shade. Divide in spring.

VERONICA Speedwell HP

Variable family with narrow
upright flower spikes 1-5 ft high,
red, pink or white, according to
variety. May-July. Need well-
drained soil. Sun or shade.
Divide autumn or spring.

YUCCA Adam's Needle   IIP

Impressive plants for specimen
positions. Long-lived once
established. Evergreen, sharp-
pointed, sword-like leaves, with
4 ft spikes of creamy-white 'bell'
flowers. July-August. Needs
sunny position and well-drained
soil. Resents disturbance. Propagate by suckers from base.

11. Selected List of Half-hardy Perennials

Begonia (Tuberous-rooted)   HHP

These tuber-forming begonias make excellent pot plants, are dazzling summer bedders in many rich colours, and are perfect for tubs, window-boxes, etc., particularly in places sheltered from strong winds. The types known as *B. pendula* are distinct in that they have slender arching and drooping growth, which makes them very suitable for hanging baskets in sheltered positions.

They all have a long flowering period, June-September, after which they must be lifted, the tops dried off and detached, and the tubers kept in dry peat in a frost-free place. The time to restart them back into growth must depend on the amount of warmth that can be provided. They need 60°F (16°C) at least, and if this is possible, a start can be made in February by setting them just at surface level in boxes of moist peat, hollow side up. A start in March, April or even early May will still give good flowering plants for summer. They must not be planted outside until towards the middle of June.

From an early start, inside shoots can be taken off and rooted as cuttings, and these will flower and make tubers of their own to keep for another year. Large tubers can also be cut into pieces, making sure each piece has a growing shoot.

Mixed colours can be grown from seed, although the seeds are very small and not easy in the early stages. Time of sowing depends on the heat available, 70°F (21°C) being needed for good germination. Plants flower in their first year, and make small tubers to keep for the following year.

Tuberous-rooted begonias.

CANNA Indian Shot   HHP

Tuber- or rhizome-forming plants, not grown on a large scale, but sometimes used as 'dot' plants in summer bedding schemes. Large leaves of varying greens and bronzes, with colourful gladiolus-like spikes of flowers from August to October.

Start dormant tubers into growth in pots or boxes, in warmth in March, plant out around mid-June. Lift in October, remove tops and store tubers in peat in frost-free place. Tubers can be divided when growth starts in spring.

Can be grown from seeds sown in warmth in spring. Seeds are hard and need soaking for 24 hours before sowing.

CHRYSANTHEMUM (Outdoor, early-flowering florist's)   HHP

Although some tougher varieties might live outside through the winter in mild districts, in general they are safer dug up in November, and kept in boxes of soil in a cold frame until January-February. They are then taken into a warm 40°-50°F (5°-10°C) greenhouse, and new plants are grown from cuttings taken from shoots springing up from the base. Old roots are not kept. Plants are gradually grown on, moved into cold frame in April for hardening off, and planted out in good soil in April-May.

A very large number of types and varieties are in existence, which give flowers of all sizes, on plants from 2-6 ft tall, in August, September and October.

Pinching out the growing tips of plants, in May, produces several branches. These can be left to grow on naturally and give sprays of flowers, or, by limiting the number of stems to 3 or 4, and by disbudding, one large bloom per stem is produced.

Plants need stakes and ties, plus feeding and protection from wind and rain to produce prize blooms, although some are weather-proof. Long-lasting when cut, and one of the best of all enthusiast's plants. New varieties raised by specialists appear every year.

DAHLIA   HHP

Tuberous-rooted plants that are blackened by the first frosts of winter, and must be dug up in October-November, and kept in a frost-free place through the winter.

Tops are cut off to within 2-3 in of tuber, and these are stored in boxes of peat or sawdust, or wrapped in newspaper and kept safe and dormant until spring. A storage place too warm and dry will cause losses from dehydration and shrivelling.

Dahlias are the most variable of all flowers. They come in all colours and colour combinations, all sizes, 1-15 in diameter flowers and all heights from 6 in to 7 ft. Single anemone-centred and double flowers, used for bedding, garden decoration, cutting and exhibition. Many new varieties appear every year.

The dahlia flowers from midsummer to the onset of frost.

Restriction of numbers of flowering stems and disbudding are necessary for exhibition blooms. Plants allowed to grow naturally flower from July to frosts, with little attention, except for staking and tying of tall varieties. Old tubers may be split up and replanted in early May or started into growth in warm greenhouse January-March, and cuttings taken and rooted, which quickly grow and come into flower. Mixed colours can be grown from seeds sown inside in March. The planting out of green plants must be delayed until danger of frost is passed – early June. Good plants and flowers for the enthusiast or the inexperienced.

GERANIUM Zonal Pelargonium   HHP

Because F1 hybrid seeds have made it possible to sow in January-February, and have flowering plants by July, this is the way more and more geraniums are being cultivated. Many are still grown, however, from cuttings taken from old plants in August-September and kept frost-free through the winter, for flowering the following year.

There are many well-established named varieties that are considered better than those raised from seeds, many with cream, gold, pink and red markings in the leaves that make them doubly attractive. Also various strains of miniatures, dwarfs, double-flowered, star-flowered and ivy-leaf trailing varieties, all in many colours and shades from white through pink, orange, red and purple. And new varieties appear every year. These of necessity have to be propagated vegetatively, which means either keeping the old plants, or taking cuttings to make new ones.

Cuttings will root at almost any time, but are best taken in July, August or September, so that they are well rooted before winter. Kept at around 40°-45°F (5°-7°C), they live as small plants, and start to regrow and flower in the spring. Old plants, if wanted, can be dug up before the frosts, potted or boxed, and kept in the same conditions. Cuttings can be taken from these when they start to grow in spring, and these will make good plants for summer, although slightly later to flower.

Zonal geraniums are ideal for bedding, or for planting in containers – window-boxes, baskets, tubs, etc. They flower best when grown in full sunlight.

GLADIOLUS   HH corms

Gladioli grow from corms, and one or two species are hardy enough to be left in the ground all winter in the warmer parts of the country. The main family, however, have to be dug up in October, kept in store through the winter, and planted out again in the spring. They are among the most showy of all flowers, coming in almost all the colours and colour combinations. The sword-like leaves may be 2-6 ft tall, according to variety and type.

The whole range is excellent for cutting from late July to September, their flowering time being partly influenced by the date of planting, which may be in March, April or May. For garden decoration, they are best planted in groups, and with the dead flowers picked off the stems regularly as they fade, they remain attractive for a long time. For best results they need deep rich soil and plenty of moisture as the flowers form.

Plant not less than 6-8 in deep, and mark planting places to avoid damage as they come through the soil. Cut down to within an inch of the corm after digging up in October, and store in single layers in boxes, in a frost-free place.

A new corm is made every year on top of the old, and these must be separated after drying, keeping the new, and throwing away the old. Small cormlets are also produced around the base. These, if kept, take 2-3 years to reach flowering size.

A number of half-hardy perennials are now only grown on a small scale, because of the time and labour involved in propagating or storing them through the winter. These include the bulbs, *Acidanthera*, ixias, some bulbous irises, ranunculus and tigridias, all of which have little chance of multiplying because of the unavoidable disturbance every year, when dug up for storing.

Popular plants of bygone days, when heating and labour were less expensive, are heliotrope, lantana, shrubby calceolaria and penstemon, often in very select named varieties. None of these is tough enough to stand the winter outside and they do not move well enough to take old plants inside. Stocks are kept by taking and rooting side-shoots as cuttings in summer and autumn, and keeping these protected over winter, for replanting the following season.

12. Selected List of Hardy Bulbs and Corms

Allium Flowering Onion

Easy to grow members of the onion family with typical onion scent. Vary from 9 in high rockery types, with yellow or pink heads of flowers, to 2-4 ft stems carrying large globes of silvery pink or lilac starry flowers in June-July. Long lasting and can be dried. Plant September-October, 6-9 in deep. Any soil.

Anemone Wind Flower

Daisy-like white, pink or blue flowers about 6 in high, growing in clumps from small tubers that quickly multiply. Good for rockeries, flowering February-April. Best in full sun. Plant 2 in deep in September. Divide when necessary.

Anemone (De Caen: Poppy Flowering)

Need a warm well-drained spot, but still tend to die away after a year or two. Large 2 in long-lasting flowers, in brilliant reds, blues and whites, on 9 in stems, excellent for cutting. Can be planted November-April to give flowers at varying times from spring to late summer.

Camassia Quamash

Easy to grow bulbs which multiply and form as a clump of strap-like leaves, with 3 ft spikes of starry white or blue flowers in June-July. Like moist and heavy soil in sun or shade. Plant September-October. Divide if necessary in autumn.

Chionodoxa Glory of the Snow

Very early 6 in high spikes of flowers, mainly blue with white eye. Also pink and white varieties. Multiply and spread easily. Plant 3 in deep September-October. Divide and replant if necessary after flowering.

Colchicum Autumn Crocus

Crocus-like mauve and pink flowers which appear from bare earth September-October. Large untidy leaves grow in spring, dying down in summer. Plant 4 in deep in July-August. Sun or shade.

Convallaria Lily of the Valley

Arching 6-9 in high sprays of fragrant white or pink bells in April-May. Spread by rhizomes underground, particularly in moisture-retaining soils and shady positions. Plant 1 in deep, September-February. Divide if necessary in September.

CROCOSMIA

Modern varieties produce sword-like leaves 4-5 ft high, with arching sprays of red, yellow or bronze flowers in August-September. Multiply readily in rich soil. Divide and replant in autumn if necessary.

CROCUS

Different species and varieties will give colour through February, March and April. Ideal for naturalising in grass or in groups in borders or rockeries. Plant 3 in deep in September-October in well-drained soil, sun or partial shade. Leaves must be left to grow after flowers fade.

CYCLAMEN

Different hardy forms of these can be planted to flower at almost any time of the year. Dwarf 4-6 in high plants with attractive marbled leaves, needing good soil and partial shade. Flowers white, pink or red. Dislike disturbance. Plant late summer. Can be grown from seed.

ERANTHIS Winter Aconite

One of the earliest of all flowers. Golden yellow 'buttercup' flowers January-March, 3 in high. Attractive in clumps under trees or large shrubs. Multiply quickly. Plant August-September, 2-3 in deep.

ERYTHRONIUM Dog's Tooth Violet

6-9 in high stems of pink or white 'star' flowers, springing from attractive leaves in March-April. Like moist soil in partial shade. Resent disturbance. Plant September-October 3 in deep. Divide if necessary in August and replant immediately.

FRITILLARIA Snake's Head

Shy pendant bells in purple and white on delicate but strong 12 in stems. Suitable for rockery or naturalising in grass. Plant September-October. Well-drained soil. Partial shade.

FRITILLARIA Crown Imperial

Large bulbs and imposing plants for specimen positions. Leaves appear in March, quickly followed by strong 3 ft stems carrying 'crown' of yellow, orange or red bells, topped with a tuft of green leaves. Plant 8-9 in deep.

Galanthus Snowdrop

Very early white flowers, January-March. Single or double, 6-12 in high, according to variety. Like partial shade. Plant 3-4 in deep, or divide and replant immediately after flowering.

Galtonia Summer Hyacinth

3-4 ft high spikes of white flowers like loose hyacinths. Resents disturbance. Plant March-April, 8-9 in deep in full sun. Multiplies steadily. Flowers August-September.

Hyacinth

Long-lasting flowers in pink, white, cream, blue and red, with strong fragrance. Good in window-boxes, tubs, etc. but rather expensive bulbs for bedding on large scale. Plant 4-6 in deep, September-October. Flowers April-May.

Iris

A large varied family that includes the border-growing types which come from rhizomes, and many that grow from bulbs. Border kinds are 1-3 ft high, according to variety, with bearded flowers in all colours. Rhizomes need dividing every 3-4 years in July-August. Bulb irises include very early-flowering (February-March) dwarf varieties, and summer-flowering (June-July) 18-24 in, grown mainly for cutting. Planting time for these is September-October in well drained soil.

Muscari Grape Hyacinth

Easy to grow and quickly multiplying bulbs, generally with blue flowers 6-9 in high, but also in pink and white. Good in groups or masses, or for ribbon borders. Any soil. Leaves can be untidy through summer. Divide in autumn when necessary.

Bearded irises.

NARCISSUS Daffodil

Most popular of all spring bulbs. Many types and varieties divided into groups by colour, length of trumpet, flowering time, number of flowers per stem, and height. Earliest will flower in March, latest in May. Height from 9-24 in. Good for all purposes, bedding, clumps in borders or naturalising. Plant September-October, 3-9 in deep, according to bulb size. Lift and divide if necessary in late summer. If moved before leaves have died down, replace in soil until dormant.

NERINE

The species *N. bowdenii* is hardy if planted in well-drained sunny spot against wall or fence. Pink heads of flowers on 2 ft high stems appear from clump of strap-like leaves in September-October. Plant bulbs 3-4 in deep in spring. Divide in spring when overcrowded, and replant at once.

SCILLA Bluebell

Common bluebells may be blue, pink or white, 9 in high, flow-

ering April-June. Sun or partial shade. Early dwarf types, generally known as scillas or squills, flower February-April, blue or white on 3-6 in stems. All multiply rapidly in most soils. Plant 2-4 in deep, August-September. Divide and replant at the same time.

TULIP

Indispensable for spring displays of any kind. Species and varieties in large numbers to suit any position. Flowering from mid-April to end of May. Different shapes, all colours, bicolours, doubles, singles, 9-30 in high, according to variety. Plant October-November, 4-6 in deep in well-drained soil. When tulips are to be followed by summer bedding, lift retaining stems and leaves and replant elsewhere until dormant. Then lift again and store dry until planting time.

Tulips as the centrepiece of a spring display.

INDEX

Italic page numbers refer to illustrations.

93